Mary Frank's Sculpture, Prints, And Drawings

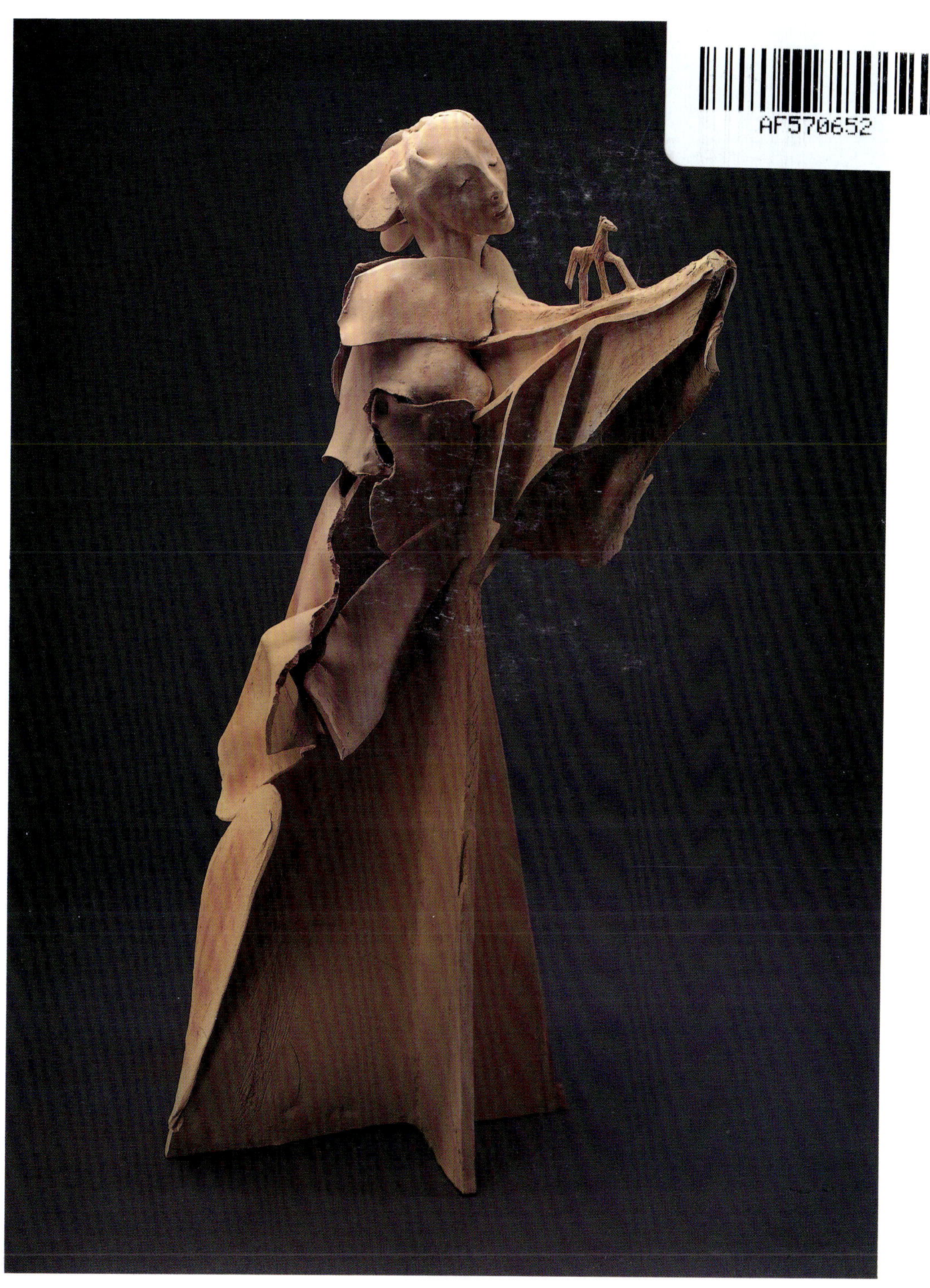

Utterance
1984
ceramic
39 1/2 x 18 x 26 inches

Mary Frank's Sculpture, Prints, and Drawings

organized by Rachel Rosenfield Lafo
Senior Curator

DeCordova and Dana Museum and Park
Lincoln, Massachusetts

February 27 - May 8, 1988

with essays by Hayden Herrera and Stella Kramrisch

DeCordova and Dana Museum and Park
Lincoln, Massachusetts
February 27 - May 8, 1988

Everson Museum of Art
Syracuse, New York
June 10 - September 4, 1988

The Pennsylvania Academy of the Fine Arts
Philadelphia, Pennsylvania
January 26 - April 9, 1989

Library of Congress catalog card no. 87-073549
ISBN: 0-945506-00-7

This exhibition and catalogue have been funded, in part, by the Art Exchange and New Works programs of the Massachusetts Council on the Arts and Humanities, a state agency.

Additional funding for the catalogue has been provided by The Sydney & Frances Lewis Foundation and Mrs. Robert M. Benjamin.

Foreword

Paul Master-Karnik, Director

One mark of the success of a work of art is its ability to impose itself upon the viewer—to make us believe in the authenticity of what the artist has experienced and to "know" that this experience is also open to us. The art of Mary Frank possesses this ability to a remarkable degree. Its impact is immediate, and readily translates across the lines of both gender and generation.

But this is not to claim that the art of Mary Frank is easy or readily accessible. Their physicality is directly felt, yet the emotional energy inspiring this impact is a product of many levels of human understanding. The title of the exhibition, **Natural Histories**, is particularly appropriate. Making reference to the general study of plant and animal life, the core of Mary Frank's art is the human figure represented in various stages of self-actualization, becoming progressively aware of an intimate and organic relation with the natural world.

It is also appropriate that the DeCordova Museum organize this important exhibition, bringing an awareness of the diversity and consistency of Frank's works to audiences in New England, and elsewhere, as the show begins its national tour. The significance of this exhibition to DeCordova has its roots in a tradition which art critic, Pamela Allara, has termed "the humanist vision of expressionist art in Boston." DeCordova has a long history of collaboration with artists who have contributed to and developed the figurative expressionist sensibility, which has characterized so much of Boston art for decades since the 1940s. It is no great mystery, for example, that among the few shows of Mary Frank's art in Boston were two during the 1960s at the Boris Mirski Gallery, which was the headquarters, as it were, of these expressionist tendencies. While arising from her own creative inspiration, and adopting no specific movement or stylistic attitude, Frank's body of work embodies the resonance of related sensibility.

Part of the unique mission of the DeCordova Museum is to place in context with developments elsewhere in America, the achievement of artists living and working in the New England region. This program of art exchange feeds the vitality of contemporary art here. Tracing the development of Mary Frank's sculpture, drawings, and prints over the past decade, **Natural Histories** also demonstrates that our distinctions among media, just as those between geographic regions, is frequently more a matter of art critical semantics than reality.

Introduction

Rachel Rosenfield Lafo
Senior Curator

On my first visit to Mary Frank's studio I was impressed with both the amount of work and the variety of media. Sculptures ranging from miniatures to human-scale standing or reclining figures made of clay, bronze, and plaster rested on the floor and shelves. Several plaster reliefs, incised and painted or embedded with clay or glass shards, were leaning on shelves. Works in other media, including metal printing plates, shadow papers, and tiny scrolls painted with watercolor were in evidence.

Since my initial encounter with Mary Frank's art it has evoked a strong response. Existing in the mythological world of her creation, figures with transported expressions and stances are charged with great intensity and longing. Without being tied to specific people or events in daily life, Mary's figures often transmit a sense of urgency, as if they are messengers bearing information of the utmost significance to the human race. The clay sculptures look as though they might have been unearthed, relics left from some unknown, ancient culture.

Mary's prints and drawings are often filled with the same intensity. Figures and animals float or run through an ethereal, timeless space. In the case of some drawings, the line is charged with such energy that the artist had to use additional sheets of paper to complete the image. She can also give us lyrical, peaceful images of landscapes and flowers. In a totally different vein the series of Holocaust prints are executed with a starkness and simplicity reflective of their mood.

Ironically, although Mary Frank's work has often been considered outside the mainstream of contemporary art, her work has been included in exhibitions in which curators, critics, and art historians explore current trends in the art scene. These include the return to figuration, the evaluation of clay as a viable material for use in the fine arts, and the focus on feminism and women's issues in the arts. But it is others who seek and find these connections. For, as much as she may be affected by events in daily life, Mary Frank remains very much her own person, responding to her own creative impulses. Characteristically, as this catalogue goes to press, she is experimenting with painting with oil on canvas and paper, unsure yet where this will lead her. It is this quest for new expressions, the tireless drive to explore new possibilities, that I believe makes her an artist of great power and distinction.

Acknowledgments

For the more than three years of planning that it took to realize this exhibition, Mary Frank gave generously of her time and energy. It has been a great privilege to work with her on this project.

An exhibition of this magnitude requires the assistance and cooperation of many individuals. I am extremely grateful to Virginia Zabriskie, Director of Zabriskie Gallery and Mary's dealer for twenty years, and to the rest of her staff, particularly Associate Director Bruce Altshuler, for their assistance with all aspects of the exhibition. The exhibition would certainly not have been possible without the cooperation of the lenders, who have generously agreed to part with their work for an extended period.

I would like to thank artist Michael Mazur for initially suggesting Mary Frank's art as the possible subject of a one-person exhibition. Dr. Hayden Herrera, art critic and lecturer, who is well known for her extensive and perceptive writings on Mary Frank's art, interviewed Mary for the videotape which accompanies this exhibition and wrote the insightful essay tracing the themes that underlie her work. I am also indebted to Dr. Stella Kramrisch, Curator Emeritus of Indian Art at the Philadelphia Museum of Art, for her intimate discussion of Mary Frank's clay sculpture. Sue Malone, Mary's assistant, was helpful in supplying the necessary details about works in the exhibition. I am grateful to Joel Meyerowitz for photographing Mary Frank for the catalogue.

We thought it important to bring Mary Frank's work to the attention of the New England public and to audiences in other parts of the country. Thus, we are delighted that the exhibition will travel to two other museums. I am grateful to Barbara Perry of the Everson Museum of Art in Syracuse, New York and Linda Bantel of the Pennsylvania Academy of the Fine Arts in Philadelphia, Pennsylvania for their support and participation in the tour of the exhibition.

Once again I have enjoyed working with designer Mark Minelli, who is responsible for the sensitive design of this catalogue. I would like to thank Geraldine Rosenfield for editorial expertise, Joseph Lafo for editorial comments, and George Vasquez and Ralph Gabriner for photography. Eric Shambroom, with the support of Video Visuals of Newton, Massachusetts, produced the videotape accompanying the exhibition.

From the beginning, I have received the support and encouragement of DeCordova Director Paul Master-Karnik and Associate Curator Lisa Weber Greenberg. I am particularly indebted to Carol Smyers for the countless hours of typing she devoted to preparing the manuscript for publication. Curatorial interns Carrie Edelstein, Lisa Saltzman, and

Gillian Titus spent much time helping on administrative and research details. Preparator Heather Lenz matted and framed works on paper and coordinated the exhibition's installation. Other museum staff members who must be thanked are Frank Balduf and Cameron Shaw for installation, Joan Sinatra Hathaway and Denise Trapani for development, and Ellen Primack for public relations.

And finally, the DeCordova Museum is grateful to the Massachusetts Council on the Arts and Humanities, a state agency, for supporting the organization of the exhibition and commissioning Hayden Herrera's catalogue essay. Additional support for the catalogue was provided by The Sydney & Frances Lewis Foundation and Mrs. Robert M. Benjamin.

R.R.L.

Mary Frank's Natural Histories

Hayden Herrera

Mary Frank's sculptures, monoprints, and drawings of the last decade celebrate an openness that is at once visceral and spiritual. It draws life in, accepts opposites and unites extremes. The openness can be joyous as in her monoprint **The Time is Now** (1985-1986) or terrifying as in her sculpture **Horse and Rider** (1982) or voluptuous as in the ceramic **Persephone** (1985). Emotion is so high-pitched that it becomes both absolutely compelling and utterly ambiguous. Is it, for example, ecstasy or pain that we see on the face of **Persephone**? Life or death in her receiving and relinquishing limbs? Either way, the urgency of Mary Frank's work draws us into a realm that we recognize as primal.

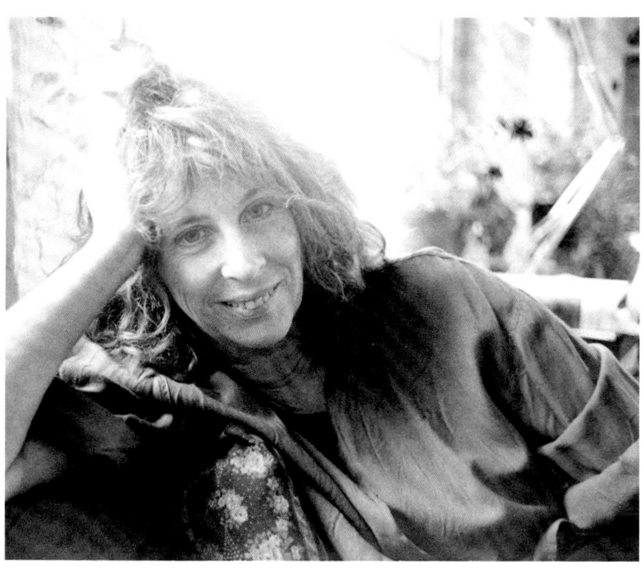

Mary Frank
in her studio,
December 1987

To enter we must shed our separateness. We must let go of mundane utility and participate in a fantasy that has the power and concreteness of myth. Here the specific touches the universal, the instant includes eternity and place becomes infinite space. A binding of flesh and spirit that is almost baroque in its extravagance directs us to our own sensuousness and vulnerability. It is perhaps this that makes Mary Frank one of the most loved of contemporary sculptors. But some are threatened by her work's openness, and they shrink back from its invitation to a more intimate contact with the self.

Openness resides in her choice and handling of materials, in the movement of line, color and shape and in her imagery. The approach is unorthodox. Plaster, glass, sticks, clay, bronze, papier mache—just about anything is used and combined to make sculpture. Similarly her works on paper employ a wide variety of materials and techniques. In 1982, perhaps inspired by **Walking Woman** and **Running Man** (1981), two life-size plaster figures into which sticks have been imbedded, she began making plaster reliefs, thus returning to a material she had used in 1967 just before turning to her chosen medium, clay. The malleability of plaster delights her. It can be cast, modelled or carved. Objects like small clay sculptures or miniature paintings on glass can be stuck into it when it is wet, and forms can be added or taken away after it has dried. Recently Mary Frank has discovered that it is a wonderful surface on which to paint in oils. In **Passage**, 1986, for example, the colors—pinks, peaches and summer greens—have a smooth, fresco-like luminosity that suits the Arcadian landscape through which two riderless horses that resemble Greek bronzes of the Geometric period roam. "The beauty of plaster," Mary Frank recently said, "is that you can go back any time, even years later, and make changes. Part of my desire to make the tablets was that I thought of them as small worlds, pieces of worlds that I could scratch into, cut into, paint, scrape off. It's also partly a desire to have a piece look as though it were a natural phenomenon. The processes are not natural ones, of course, but the pieces have lived through a certain period of time and they bear the imprint of what I've done to them." [1]

Another material to which Mary Frank has recently returned is bronze. In the 1950s she modelled small figures in wax and had a few of them cast in bronze. Then in the 1960s, she cast some of her plasters depicting a woman standing in or before the sea. But the expense prevented her from casting many works. In the 1980s, with a number of museum shows behind her and a large following of devoted patrons, she has been able to have several clay sculptures cast. The most spectacular is a large bronze bust of a woman cast in 1986 from a 1984 sculpture. Head tilted back, eyes closed, mouth open, the woman offers herself to and drinks in the surrounding world. For all her fleshy substance, her vivid blue patina makes her seem a concretization of air. The story of her making has an openness as well. Before the clay head could dry, the temperature in Mary's studio fell below freezing. Cracks opened up on the woman's cheeks and forehead and slowly moved towards her eyes and mouth. "They had their own beauty, but I knew I would have to destroy the piece. One day the sculptor Alan Siegel dropped by and suggested that I cast it. So I did. I never would have thought of it myself," she says. [2]

In recent years Mary Frank has become increasingly engaged in making monoprints, prints made by painting on the inked metal plate using a brush, finger, rag, or any other implement, and then pulling the print through the press. She has a large variety of stencils cut out of paper or metal which she places on the plate, inks, and sometimes flips over or moves so that the same figure will appear in reverse or in another position in the same print or in an entirely different print. When the stencils have accrued many layers of paint through years of use, they may reappear in collages. Her printmaking process has become so complex that even Mary Frank is not always able to tell how certain effects were achieved.

She works in series, re-inking and changing the plate so that each of some six or seven prints is unique. "I love the possibility of having the past, present and future at the same time. In sculpture when you make a change you lose what you had before. Working in a series, you try to keep the image alive as long as possible, but all the work has to be

[1] Margaret Moorman, "In a Timeless World," *Artnews*, Vol. 86, May, 1987, p.94.

[2] All quotes unless otherwise noted are from conversations with Mary Frank in her New York studio on September 28 and 29, 1987

done in one long session on one day, otherwise the ink will dry. Because of the time element I work in a kind of frenzy. There is a lot of preparation and planning, but I change things in response to what I see happening on the plate. When I make a series, there isn't a logical progression from dark to light. By re-inking and wiping parts out, often the fourth print is dark again. There's so much possibility of adding or subtracting, entrances and exits. Sometimes 'ghosts' (images that turn up again in paler versions after the first printing) disappear and then reappear unexpectedly later on. The process is an enormous layering of ways of working, of ideas and sudden violent shifts of feeling."

In the last few years Mary Frank has also made paintings on metal. Instead of cleaning and reusing her metal plates, she keeps them, sometimes changing them slightly, and hangs them on her studio wall. She takes pleasure in the accumulated history of decisions suspended like a palimpsest in these plates—the inkings, re-inkings, the jostlings, juxtapositions and transformations. As art objects, these plates are curious in that the decisions involved in their making were focused not on the plates themselves, but on the prints pulled from them. But their beauty seizes us as it did their maker. "I began looking at the plates, and I decided that the plate was more interesting than the print. Sometimes I throw the print away. I love the color of the metal coming through the paint." The light that glows from behind forms is in perfect accord with the subjects depicted—nudes, birds, plants, all manner of life, floating in a kind of celestial ether, a volatile substance that is like the sensation of air thickening when life is heightened by some extreme happiness such as the recognition of beauty or being in love.

Mary Frank draws on anything that strikes her fancy: leaves, mushrooms, color-graded paint chips, rolls of paper used for taping walls. She draws on clay plaques with iron oxide or glazes. Two years ago she molded handmade paper into a relief and then painted on it. She makes collages, rubbings and "shadow papers" in which the lines she cuts into white paper depict figures, when seen against light. In a series of lovers, lines of light quivering with shadow perfectly describe this tremulous state.

Mary Frank spends as much or more time drawing from her finished sculptures as drawing for them. Her 1987 exhibition at The Brooklyn Museum revealed the way she takes a theme, in this case Persephone, and explores it in a large number of works on paper. "If I've made a sculpture and then draw it, I see that sculpture differently," she once said. "And then, from that, sometimes I may make other sculptures." [3] Mary Frank also draws from her imagination, sometimes she even jots down images seen in dreams.

[3] Paul Cummings, "Interview: Mary Frank Talks with Paul Cummings," *Drawing*, May-June, 1981, p.11.

To keep her hand and eye true, to keep from falling into style, she often draws from life. Her bold charcoal sketches or drawings in brightly colored inks capture the gestures of models as they move about her studio. She thinks of her models as collaborators, not passive objects: "For twenty-five years," she says, "I have worked together with my friend the dancer Luly Santangelo. She brings such a full range of expression to movement that it is a challenge to equal her intensity." Mary also draws from animals at the zoo, fish in aquariums, plants at the New York Botanical Gardens, or in her own lush garden in the Catskills. Over the years she has made many sketches of actors at the Open Theater and other theatrical companies. In the summer she can be seen walking slowly down the beach while drawing in one of her small notebooks which form a visual diary.

Drawing for her is a way of keeping in touch with the world. "It's a way of seeing. There is drawing for the sheer pleasure of drawing and then drawing as part of a journal. My notebooks are very important to me. Sometimes I forget about drawings I've made in them, and then these images show up later somewhere else."

Typical of Mary Frank's openness is her feeling that all of her media are intimately related. "There's a lot of exchange between them. They learn from each other. I often draw in a very physical way. I'm using my hand a lot, not just the point of a pencil or a pen. It often feels very sculptural. When I cut lines into paper to make shadow papers, or when I'm drawing it feels three dimensional even though it's flat. Clay is wonderful to draw in. When I choose a medium, the decision comes out of a certain urgency. The medium I've been using no longer works for me."

Mary Frank is best known as a sculptor working in clay, a material perfectly suited to the fluency of her vision. Nothing is closed or static in her work. Everything is in flux, as cheek flows into shoulder or arm into wing, and bodies metamorphose into earth, air, water, animals or trees. Always there is the sense that her creatures are coming into being, just taking form in ink or clay. Their shapes result from a spontaneous give and take between the movements of her body and the body of her clay. Form does not seem imposed, but, of course, to a great extent it is. Truth to materials is all very well, she points out, but gravity-seeking clay is apt to slouch into an amorphous clump if left to its own devices. It is Mary Frank's genius that she can let clay look like clay while at the same time transforming it so that it responds to the slightest leap of her imagination.

As with her monoprints, Mary Frank's method of building a sculpture involves a mixture of plan and improvisation. After rolling the clay out into flat slabs, she cuts, tears, molds, props, folds and drapes the slabs to create figures. Deliberately she leaves spaces between and under the slabs so that structure is open and parts have room to breath. In larger pieces clay slabs form an architectural armature over which the more organic sections of the figure are laid. "The armature gives certain thrusts to the piece," she explains. "The initial structure has the bones. I like to be able to see it, and I don't know in advance how much of it will be covered up."

In the early 1970s, because she could not fit a life-size figure in her kiln, she began to assemble large clay figures out of a number of sections. When she laid the pieces out on the ground, sometimes the parts touched and sometimes they did not. Many people saw these figures as fragmented, but Mary saw the sections as part of a single flow of energy. The interstices between forms were alive for her. "I don't think of them as voids," she comments. The figures are often incomplete, but missing hands or feet do not seem amputated. Rather they merge with their surroundings. "I needed to make a figure with a lot of space inside it and a lot outside," Mary Frank says. "The space moves back and forth like a kind of breathing." Space flows into form, and form flows out into space as naturally as light moving among leaves or water through rocks at a stream's bottom. It pulls us in. In works like **Woman with Petal Arms**, 1980, or **Chant**, 1984, this mingling of space and form suggests a coupling. Etched on the women's thighs are lines that track space's movement. These lines also declare sensation, tracing its impulse on flesh. But the spaces between forms can also suggest the tug of mortality, flesh sinking into and merging with earth.

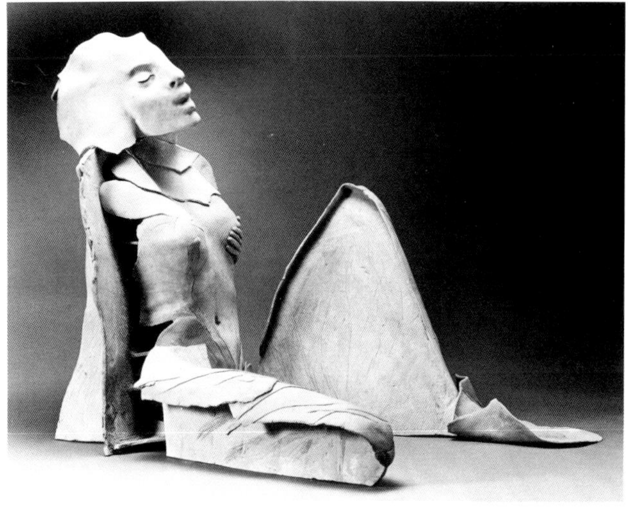

Chant
1984
ceramic
44 x 38 x 60 inches

Collection of Virginia Museum of Fine Arts: Gift of the Sydney and Frances Lewis Foundation.

Mary Frank's figures of women share certain characteristics that make them archetypal. They have, for example, their own peculiar kind of vitality and grace as they move through space. Unlike her male figures, who most often ride, run or leap toward some goal, they seem to be in a state of harmony with nature. Their beautiful and sensuous faces are caught in a trance that recalls the anguished rapture of Bernini's open-mouthed closed-eyed St. Teresa. This transport is clearly erotic. It is also sexual in the broadest sense—it describes an embracing of life.

Mary's women have been seen as imaginary self-portraits, and it is true that they do capture the artist's creature-like quality, the intensity of her physical presence and her peculiar alertness to the world. But she sees them as coming from a time before people divided into races. She suspects that the origin of her women's features could be a photograph she saw as a child in a copy of the magazine **Verve** that she found in the studio of her mother, the painter Eleonore Lockspeiser. "It was a quickly-made terracotta doll's head from India with deep, lidded, half-open eyes and an open mouth. Imagine the poignancy of this face. I seem to have absorbed it. It has stayed in that place behind my eyes, and it keeps on reappearing."

If the source of her woman's physiognomy cannot be pinpointed, neither can the woman's personality or type. She is everywoman. "Often I've been asked where sources come from," Mary Frank said last June in a commencement speech at the Boston Museum School. "For me, they're from direct observation, from drawing from models for many, many years. Drawings of people, animals, plants, water, fire, movement, but also from imagination and states of being. What I feel it is to be human. What life on earth is, or might be. It is very important for me to find a vocabulary or series of images that feel strong enough to put all the feelings I have in. Sometimes I have the image of a ship that could be loaded up and could move through time." [4] Mary Frank's woman is like that ship. She is strong enough to carry the cargo of feeling. "I like it when people bring a lot of their own lives to the pieces," Mary says. "I want to make something that allows various readings."

The faces of her women are, Mary allows, "in a state—maybe a state of grace, not necessarily in the Christian sense, but in a sense that is conveyed by the Yiddish saying: 'Out of longing, and out of song, time was created. And, there is just enough time for one more day.' I want to make that state of grace palpable." The women's faces express a perfect equilibrium between inner feeling and awareness of what is happening outside the self—the same inside/outside equivalence that we saw in her figures' open structure. **Persephone**, for example, seems to listen to the promptings of her dark underworld even as she rejoices in the sensations of rain, sun, wind and earth that touch her from the world without.

When she is working well, Mary Frank's creative process is open and improvisational. "I often have a very definite idea," she says, "but the minute you touch the work, it can change. The hand has its own life. It makes marks and gestures which are not deliberate. I often think of them as tracks of animals. There is a dialogue between materials and

[4] Mary Frank, Commencement speech at the Boston Museum School, transcript, Mary Frank's personal archive.

the original intention that is both a pleasure and a warfare." Mary Frank accepts chance and accident, but there is nothing passive in her approach. She is so knowledgeable about the behavior of her materials and so sure of her vocabulary of form that she can create situations in which certain kinds of "accidents" will occur. "Accidents are *your* accidents," she says. "To some degree you can feel them coming, so you harness them or throw them out." Being open to chance is a way of keeping her imagery and style alive and changing. Of the drawings she makes at rehearsals or performances, she has said, "Working in the dark has made me do drawings I could not otherwise have done. By not being able to see, I take chances and follow other intuitions." There is a kind of muscle memory that guides her fingers across the paper. Having to trust it makes the contact between form seen and drawn even more concrete. But this open approach means there is a high mortality rate in her art. Firing is often traumatic, for many pieces break or change in the kiln, and she throws a large number of her drawings and prints away.

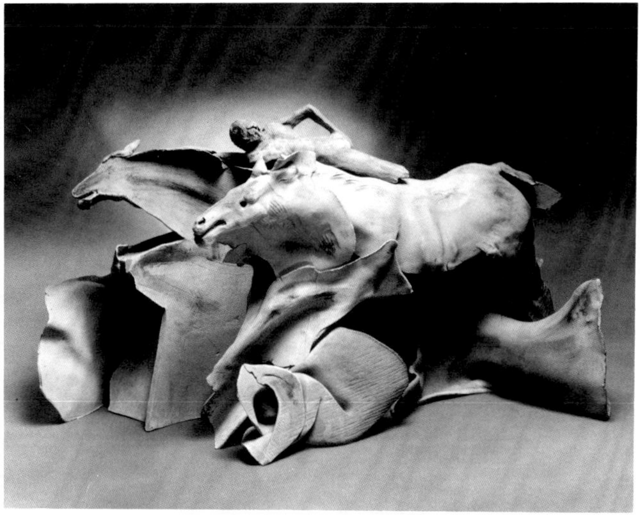

Horse and Rider,
1982
ceramic
24 x 43 x 31 1/2 inches

Part of the shape and meaning of **Horse and Rider** was found in the process of working. "In the beginning," Mary recalls, "it was one horse, and then the horses pulled apart." When Mary makes a sculpture out of a number of sections, the various pieces can shift positions until she settles on a final arrangement. Like Rodin, she sometimes makes various limbs for a figure before deciding on one that feels right. In the case of **Horse and Rider**, she tried out four or five different riders. The slight, nude equestrian she chose looks back over his shoulder with an expression of horror, as if he were escaping a tidal wave. The rhythm of his half-swimming, half-running motion does not keep pace with the horse's runaway momentum. Speed is accentuated by clouds of turbulence that define space for thundering hooves. The rider can hardly keep his mount, and the feeling of crisis is intensified by the horse's splitting so that one half veers away from ands pulls ahead of the other. To hold the galloping horses together, the rider stretches his right arm across the widening chasm. There are handprints where he tried and failed to get a grip on the other side of the horse's neck.

The motif of the horse and rider, a metaphor for the journey through life, has always attracted Mary. In her early bronzes and in many drawings, the journey seems lighthearted, even playful. In **Horse and Rider** it is a struggle for survival: life is a headlong dash towards death. Indeed the horse or horses appear to be consuming their own life energy by a speed they cannot halt. Ribs protrude and eyes are skeletal hollows. As an image of crisis, **Horse and Rider** comes, like all of Mary Frank's work, directly out of her life. The period in which she made it was one full of conflict, pain and upheaval.

But Mary Frank is reticent about discussing sources in her personal life, and she prefers to talk about discoveries made while the piece was in progress and after. "Because of torsion and pressure from fire in the kiln, the horses moved apart. It could have destroyed the piece. The figure might not have been able to span the gap." The other surprise was Mary's recognition of the relationship between **Horse and Rider** and an experience she had had ten years before: "After finishing it I realized that it was like being at Canyon de Chelly in Arizona. I walked at the bottom of the canyon and looked up, and I sat on the edge and saw the shadow of a crow below me on the canyon wall. Then I heard the crow, and after what seemed a long time, I saw it. I wanted **Horse and Rider** to have this same kind of awe. You don't often know what your sources are, what's drawing you or what's pulling you. At the time, I tried to draw and make sculptures of the canyon, but **Horse and Rider**, made ten years later, is closer to my experience."

When in her monoprints, arms and legs come loose and fly about by themselves or turn up attached to some other body, it is oneness, not dividedness that is communicated. At other times splitting can express urgency as in the **Running Man** (1981) drawn on two separate pieces of clay so that he must take a running leap to get across the chasm. When Mary splits her sculpted heads she does not destroy their unity, rather she unites the heads with space. The first split head was **Conceciao Aparecido**. "I was not happy with this head," Mary recalls. "She looked both old and young. I decided to destroy it by cutting it in half with a wire. And then by being willing to give the piece up as lost, I found something."

The heads from the 1980s continue a long series from the previous decade, but they seem less funebral, more given to life. **Head with Running Figure** (c. 1982) is sheared off down the middle so that one half is a molded face of an open-mouthed woman and the other half is flat. On the flat side, the silhouette of a running man could be a thought or dream running through the woman's mind or perhaps the sheer momentum of feeling.

Hands drawn to movement as eyes to fire or to ocean waves, Mary Frank tries to catch the momentary gesture that speaks of something elemental–a woman holding her breasts, a man leaping. Even her standing figures are never engaged in the prosaic gestures of everyday life such as picking up a cup of coffee or hailing a taxi. "I tend to like work that has an urgent quality to it," she admits, but that urgency is never bound by purpose. When she was young she studied dance with Martha Graham, and the movements Mary depicts have a Graham-like intensity, and an understanding of how movement feels from deep inside the body. Indeed, much of her figure's emotive force comes from our kinesthetic empathy with their postures.

In this they are like dancers—and some are dancers. At once impulsive and ceremonial, **Sufi Dancer** (1980-81) and **Three Dancers** (1981) are like priests and priestesses who dance to stir the forces that give life. In her commencement address, Mary told the students about a West African dance that she had seen. "The gestures of the dance go like this," she said. "They go from the heart, to the sky, to the gods, to the rain, to the sun. They go back to the heart and to the beloved, back to the heart and to the earth, back to the heart and to the four directions, six really, including up and down. Back to the heart twice and then they bow deeply to the drummers who make the dance possible. I mention this because of the repetition, which I find beautiful. It is urgent and there is no indifference or irony towards any of these that are being saluted." She could have been describing her own work, its incantatory mood, its lack of "indifference or irony."

Besides the movement implied in a figure's action, there is the abstract movement of clay and of space, line, light and shadow. Mary Frank's sculptures also change in the most unpredictable ways as the spectator moves around them. The back of a walking woman, for example, may turn out to be a sheared off surface upon which a nude is profiled. In addition, the movements involved in making a piece are left clearly in in evidence: fingers dragged through clay, or a rag wiped across a monoprint plate, give the work an immediacy that is powerfully engaging. Finally Mary sees an equivalence between motion and emotion: "The impulse to work comes from being moved, a word I take literally. Maybe that's why I draw moving animals or people. Their movement gives an image to my own. I mean, when we say we are moved, something is actually changing in us."

As figures move through space, they take space with them. **Walking Woman**'s (1980) step forward is carried into waves of drapery, into striations scratched on her sides and into a hood-like structure that

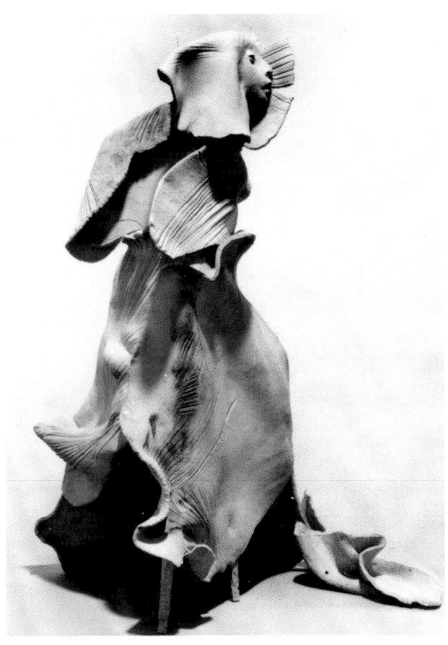

Walking Woman
1980
ceramic
31 x 23 x 13 inches

forms a transition between her face and the currents of air it stirs as she moves. Her advance is so persuasive that the viewer forgets that her anatomy is almost as abstract as that of Boccioni's striding man in **Unique Forms of Continuity in Space** (1913). Unlike the space in a drawing or monoprint, Mary Frank points out, "the space around a sculpture is limitless." She takes that boundlessness and gives it concrete life.

She does not give it specificity. As with her faces and gestures, space is not pinned down to a particular locale. She eschews the logic of Western perspective, preferring to see space as infinite extension. Jumps in scale do not necessarily mean changes in distance. Like primitive artists—or like Picasso—Mary Frank is apt to make something large because it is important to her. Or it could be that she has imaginatively entered the space of her work and approached a motif from the other side. Extreme scale jumps can also occur because of the odd vantage point from which she sometimes draws. "On the beach in Cape Cod I like to dig a hole in the sand and lay my face in it so that I can get closer to the horizon. I might see my own hand or somebody else's leg nearby, and next to them I see a tiny figure walking at the edge of the ocean way down the beach. I draw the figure tiny and the knee large because that's how it looked to me." Mary's is an emotional way of conceiving space and scale. The small horse that walks towards the end of a woman's outstretched arm in the wonderfully eloquent **Utterance** (1984) was, she says, like a painful memory that she was both relinquishing and cherishing. "Depth is not only deep space, it's also time. What comes forward and what recedes."

The space and time surrounding figures in monoprints appear to go on forever. "The time is now," she says, but now includes millenia. She does not think of depth as the measurable position of objects in a given volume of space. Usually there is no horizon line in her works on paper. "For years," she recently told a critic, "I drew nudes that could've been in the air. I never drew the chair or the horizon or whatever else there was in the picture. I knew it was there, of course, but I didn't recognize it as something that should be a mark on paper. Then at one point I felt I had discovered the horizon, like someone who 'discovers' the umbrella—as if it hadn't been around all along. It was like discovering gravity—it put everybody on terra firma." [5]

In spite of that "discovery," many of the works on paper have a seamless expanse of space, from front to back, from top to bottom. Or sometimes there are two horizon lines in one image. In **Passage** a horizon line is inserted in what should be the middle distance in order to

[5] Margaret Moorman, op. cit., p.92

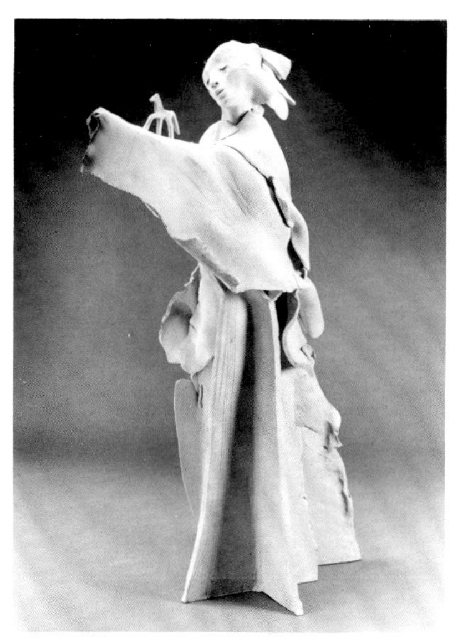

Utterance
1984
ceramic
39 1/2 x 18 x 26 inches

give a horse a place to walk. This wayward approach to space may seem childlike, but it is also a deliberate rejection of conventions. Equally wayward and purposeful is Mary Frank's disregard of the rectangular limits of her paper. When she draws, her focus on her motif is so consuming that figures are frequently cut off by the framing edge. In the dramatic and fiercely sexual drawing of **Persephone** (1985), for example, the nude needed to be complete but there was no more room on the sheet, so Mary grabbed another and then another to give her figure room to live. This adding of sheets of paper to create an irregularly shaped drawing surface is the sculptor's prerogative: when she builds figures she adds clay until the body takes its own space.

Space in the monoprints and paintings on metal plates is created by the movement of light, color and texture. In many prints it is structured by the marks of the roller rolling ink onto the plate. These marks create a loose grid like the squares of gold leaf that form the background in Japanese screens. In the screen-like **The Time is Now**, a six-part monoprint in which each vertical panel has a separate leaping nude, the roller marks play against an oceanic tumult of reds and blues so that the figures are surrounded not by a void but a firming up of space—what Mary Frank calls a "firmament." Space projects out from the figures and is determined by their motion and emotion; figures and space are of one substance.

"The piece started as a single figure and developed over a number of weeks," Mary recalls. Her mood was buoyant and clay dragged down by gravity could not express the springiness she felt. "I can't do figures in air in sculpture so I do them a lot in drawings and prints," she says. The two male figures are made from the same stencil. In the second panel, the man is paler and more transparent. Birds have been added and he has an extra leg to indicate movement. Similarly, the woman leaping upwards toward light in the third panel is a "ghost" of the bright blue nude in the fifth panel. The repetition and the change from highly saturated color to a paler, translucent echo reaffirm the notion that all time is encompassed in the instant.

"**The Time is Now** was an attempt to create a sense of being in the moment," Mary Frank observes. "Space is like a stellar perspective. It's an expression of the figures' state of feeling." The viewer can be transported to this horizonless, gravity-free perspective and feel the figures' leap in his or her own body. The "firmament" where these figures dance is, Mary says, "a substance or a place where people can be transformed—by color, by light, often by sound. By experience. By love." [6]

[6] Margaret Moorman, op. cit., p.92

Mary Frank's capacity for joy is equalled by her capacity for grief. Not long after she produced **The Time is Now** she made a series of monoprints on the theme of the Holocaust. In contrast to the vivid color and exuberant movement of the airborn nudes, this series is starkly black, white and gray. Life is at a standstill. The series was prompted by a fleeting image that Mary saw on television. "It was a photograph of bodies from a concentration camp piled on a cart and covered with snow. In a Japanese book I saw photographs of the Siege of Leningrad with dead bodies in the streets in the snow. Two years later I did this series of monoprints. It was very difficult for me. I felt the subject was taboo. The bodies in the cart waiting to be buried is the ultimate image of abandonment. When it snows, it snows on everything."

Printed on rice paper that seems as evanescent as the bodies is the image of the cart that haunted her. Sometimes it is juxtaposed with a portrait of a gaunt, shaven woman prisoner who stares the stare of death in life. In this series, Mary's usually fluent and searching hand has foregone the impulsive swoops and dashes that impell her drawings of nudes and flowers. Lines as spare and stiff as her subject etch out shapes in a way that is uncharacteristically literal. It is as if the artist felt it would be wrong to indulge her transforming imagination.

Her procedure was simple. She inked the plate, lay a sheet of paper face down on it and drew on the back of the paper with a pencil, a fork or her fingernail. "I started working blindly," she wrote. "My fingernails felt their way on the back of the paper transferring black marks from the inked plate underneath. The subject was teaching me." [7]

As a politically engaged artist, Mary Frank has produced posters or given works to support various causes. With the exception of the Holocaust series, her expressions of rage and pain at humanity's inhuman treatment of life on this earth have generally been oblique. A sculpture of a mother with a dead child was one of many sculptures made in response to the Vietnam massacres. In **Crouching Woman with Two Faces** (1981) a woman holds a plant as protectively as if it were a child to which she had just given birth. Mary Frank is particularly passionate about environmental issues: "If we are the highest form of life—and I don't know if we really are—it is our responsibility to protect where we live on this planet, and it is the opposite of what we're doing. I mean the hummingbird and the elephant are not destroying the planet. We are." The crouching earth-mother enfolding two leaves that might be the last leaves on earth is a kind of idol dedicated to the survival of life.

[7] *Mary Frank: Sculpture and Works on Paper*, exhibition catalogue, Zabriskie Gallery, New York, 1986, n.p.

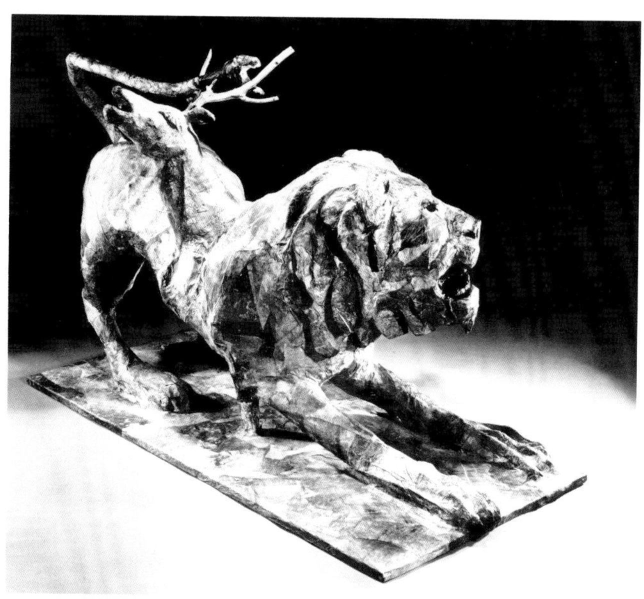

Chimera
1984-86
papier mache
34 x 60 x 24 inches

If the crouching nude is an idol, **Chimera** (1983-1986) is an omen. Part lion, part antelope, part serpent, this fabulous monster is made out of papier mache as if to emphasize its fragility and its chimerical quality, for a chimera has no substance except in the imagination. Mary Frank first saw a chimera in a book on Etruscan art that she found in her mother's painting studio. "I took the book to bed with me even though the image frightened me. Forty years later, in Florence, I saw the bronze Chimera. It was more terrifying but it was even more amazing. I started to make a chimera. I made the insides with wood, metal, and chicken wire, with cloth, plaster and paper. Using old, crumpled black, gray and red rice paper monoprints I made its outer skin. I like the way the prints composted into the sculpture. It was many-colored once. Though the antelope is the tender aspect, I did not want to give it a humble color." [8]

In using old monoprints as compost to make the creature's body, Mary alludes to the idea of death fertilizing life. The roaring **Chimera**, with the antelope's head painted red as a wound bursting from its back and with its lion's tail turned serpent biting the antelope's horns is a vivid image of cycles of life and death. "It signals the destruction of the earth," Mary says, "but it's not only a metaphor. It really is a chimera. When I make figures, they are figures, not metaphors, though they do embody certain meanings or states of being." For a long time the **Chimera** had no tail. "I couldn't bring myself to finish the tail, to make the serpent's head," she once said. "I found it so depressing, so terrible, so I just left it blank."[9] When she finally added the snake, the agent of the Fall, **Chimera** became a kind of Adam and Eve image for the nuclear age.

Mary Frank does not see her political involvement as anything unusual. "Today there's no way a person could not be affected by the environment, by Aids, or by the threat of nuclear disaster. You can't help but use these things in art. If your eyes are open only to your work and closed to life around you, the work will suffocate. It is difficult to work with these concerns—to make a piece about the Vietnam war, for example, and have it feel authentic, not like rhetoric."

Many of Mary Frank's pieces, for example a group of works based on Botticelli's **Primavera** that she made five years ago, refer to past art. Her sources are myriad: cave paintings, Egyptian and Greek sculpture, Pre-Columbian and Oriental art, primitive art of all kinds. Degas and

[8] Ibid.

[9] Margaret Moorman, op. cit., p.94.

Rodin have been fertile influences, and in the twentieth century she has looked hard at Giacometti, Henry Moore, Reuben Nakian, and of course at Picasso. "There are artistic sources, and there are life sources. Sometimes I don't know one from the other. It could be something I've seen or heard. Music has always been a great source for me. I listen to music a lot while I work. I'm influenced by things I've read. Friendships with other artists are important. Peter Schumann's Bread and Puppet Theater and Margaret Israel's sculpture have been particularly inspiring. Indigenous art is a great source. Often I recognize an influence only after a piece is finished. When I look at art I am bowled over—I mean, the human imagination is of great beauty."

Although she is touched by many influences both in the art of the past and the present, Mary Frank is essentially on her own. Her work bears very little relationship to anything else that is happening in contemporary art. When asked if the current Neo-expressionist trend had anything to do with the heated color and greater painterliness of her work in recent years, Mary gives her interlocutor a withering silent frown. Perhaps because of her emphasis on the direct and spontaneous communication of feeling rather than on devising new ways of organizing form, Mary Frank's work has not developed in a simple progression from one stylistic period to the next. She often goes back and uses ideas or subjects from years before, and her approach is inclusive—there is no reason why she can't work in several somewhat different modes at the same time or even in the same piece. Yet all of her work is immediately recognizable as hers; it is as close to her as her own face. And, though there is no programmatic formal development, there are changes over the years that make it possible to know more or less to what years a given piece belongs.

In general, the sculpture has become more complex and more subtle. If we compare, for example, **Rainbow Woman** (1972) to the untitled woman with arched back from 1981, the move away from primitivism and toward complexity is obvious. The integration of the architectural armature with the organic curves of the figure has become more intricate and sculpturally more expressive, and transitions between forms—say a leg moving into a torso, or a forehead into hair—are less abrupt, more nuanced.

The most pronounced change in the work of the 1980's is its luxuriant color. "I felt a real need for more color in my work," she says. "It was like a primal need. Color is so new; it has been a great struggle. I was addicted to black and white. In a way it was satisfying because black and white contained all the colors. It seemed so difficult to find the colors to express a state of being." Mary Frank paints on her plaster reliefs as if they were canvases, and, inspired perhaps by the brilliant patina of her bronze head, she has gone so far as to paint **Ethiopian** and **Woman in Wave, Spring**, (both 1986-1987) with various shades of blue. In monoprints she has expanded into a full range of color that is no longer dominated by its relation to black. The imaginative freedom of her color choices is expressionist. "Color," she says, "is related to the natural world, but not necessarily to the subject that I'm depicting. For example, I might see the color of a leaf under ice, and that color might turn up later maybe on a horse." Most recently her obsession with color has led her to turn to painting in oil on canvas.

The highly saturated color of many of her monoprints reflects her happier state of mind—that same ebullience expressed in **The Time is Now** and other prints of airborn creatures. To have companionship and continuity, to love and to be loved is an occasion for joy—it has not always been so; Mary Frank's life has been full of loss and longing. Her contentment is revealed also in an abundance of flowers—tulips, poppy fields, bouquets seen and imagined glowing with an almost otherworldly light. "The flowers," she avows, "are explosions of color, and they are probably connected to living with a man I love." She refers to the well-known musicologist Leo Treitler.

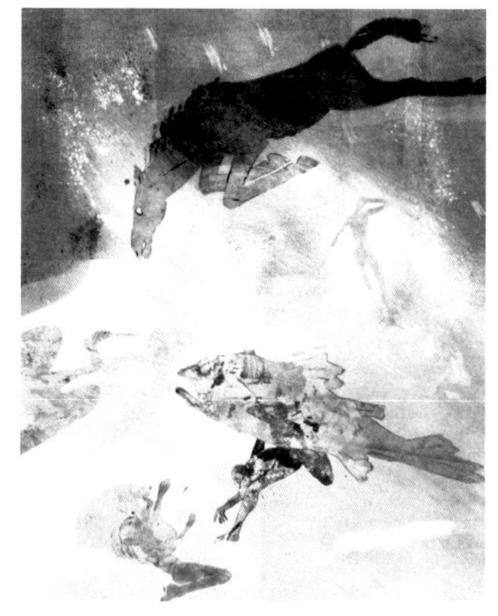

Leap
1984
monoprint on paper
36 x 27 7/8 inches

The work of the 1980s is populated also by a great array of animals. There appears to be no division between the kingdoms of creatures, plants and human beings. "When people ask me why I depict animals, I always want to ask them why they don't put animals in their work. We are still sharing the earth with animals, though many are becoming extinct. Unfortunately, I guess, we're not sharing the earth, we are controlling or destroying it."

In a number of monoprints from the mid-1980s, for example, **Leap** (1984), people, horses, herons, fish, snakes and geese—even centaurs—sail through the "firmament" in an apocalyptic vision that could be the beginning or the end of the world. These prints have titles like **Origins** (1984) or **Natural History** (1985): they depict the evolution of life not as biology exactly, but as vision. In her commencement address, Mary quoted the Spanish architect Gaudi's statement that "originality is the return to origins," and she went on to advise: "I feel it is important to respect all the parts of yourself, some of which are from before speech, and are connected to your desire toward form, color, images, materials, your need to take risks and the playfulness that is in you from birth." Prints such as **Centaur** acknowledge these primal parts of the artist's self, her primitive urge toward form and color, towards life. In **Natural History** a leaping man, red with desire, races towards a crimson woman who kneels with outstretched arms on the opposite side of the long horizontal sheet. A fish, a leaping horse and a blue leaping man who could be the same suitor at a different moment in time, join in the trajectory that might signal the beginning of evolution. A series of prints depict the overlapping shadows of a giant heron and a running man, as if this were a kind of mating, and the bird's shadow sometimes takes human form. Similarly, in an earlier series, a man leans down to touch his shadow which has the profile of a horse, or in **Recognition**, 1984, a nude woman moves towards an ibex, which she sees as another aspect of herself. Birds and horses commingling with people create a mythic ambiance in which all creatures carry within them the origins and future of life.

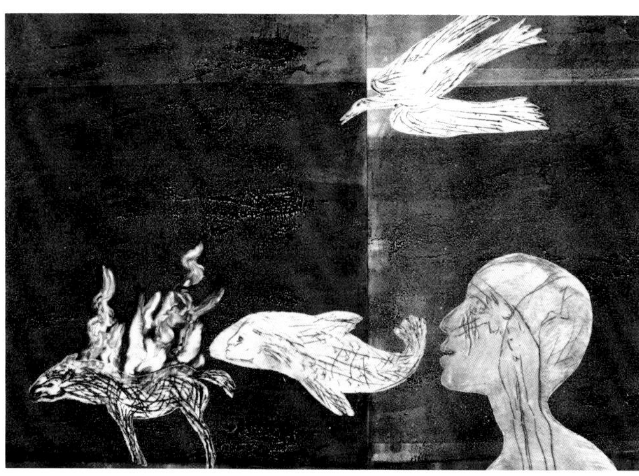

The Storm is Here
1982
Monoprint and drypoint on paper
23 3/4 x 35 1/4 inches

If there is a future. In **The Storm is Here** (1982), a series of some twenty or thirty monoprints taken from several plates (in some parts of which she uses drypoints as well) the evolution and destruction of life is played out using the print as stage. "It's like a theater with entrances and exits," Mary observes. "It's about the horror of what's being done to this earth."

The cast of characters in **The Storm is Here** includes the profile of a man's head sometimes inscribed with the figure of a woman, a walking woman, a winged woman, a crawling man, a running man (taken from the large plaster figure of 1981) a skeleton, plants, the sun, dinosaurs and a primordial horse that occasionally bursts into flame. In many prints a crowd of gesticulating humans flees from some unseen horror. As the masses huddle together their bodies dissolve and become a mass that resembles a rock cliff. Whatever the storm is that frightens them, that storm is here. Just as **The Time is Now** is an invitation to live more fully in the present, **The Storm is Here** is a warning that the theater of life may close.

Clay Sculpures by Mary Frank

Stella Kramrisch

Mary Frank creates mythic beings. They exist in the clay of her sculptures. They tell and have no story, no past, no place except their form which is tangible, tactile and touching, brought about by the magic touch of the sculptor's hand that impresses her inwardness on the earth. The earth is material which she forms and transforms. The shape of her figures is basically heavy with the weight of the earth.

The element water liquefies the earth, softens the clay, imparts fluidity to the contours of the sculpture. In Mary Frank's hands earth and water are elemental, active substances. They acquire the form that her creative intelligence imparts to them: weighty solidity, flowing contours and cavities. Her figures of myth evolve as she shapes them.

Her shapes are allusive. They are clay in its several modalities of form. One of these is the slab produced by flattening the lump of clay with a rolling pin. In slab shape clay sheds most of its bulk but remains malleable and can be bent in convex and concave planes. These can be cut or torn, smooth edged or ragged. By its technical adaptability clay itself can assume an iconographical function and become part of the mythical image.

Clay slabs flattened become sheaths when molded by Frank on a volumetric body. Laid on the modelled shape, then lifted from it, they take over its volume though not its bulk. They are movable and each claims attention as they are laid out next to though separated one from the other. Together with their intervals they form a whole larger than the parts of the original figure, for their intervals divide as much as they connect them. The contemplating eye fills the gaps between the single shards, their fragmentation conjures original continuity, and a new concept of form arises in which the separated, and as if scattered, parts clamor to form a part of a larger whole.

A favorite subject in Frank's works is the embrace of lovers. Her entire work is pervaded by the presence of the god, Kama, whom Indian myth describes as bodiless (Ananga), diffused in all that lives. Kama is desire, love, the love of God. Whatever their subject, Mary Frank's sculptures embody this god.

The tension and counterpoint of paradoxical coordinated qualities, ponderous substantiality and weightless void, are heightened when the hollow clay shell which retains the modelled amplitude of the solid earthen shape breaks up, exposing its chasms and hollowness. The range of earthen form comprises in one sculpture the antithetic though inherent qualities of earth in its sculptural transformation. Kama, the

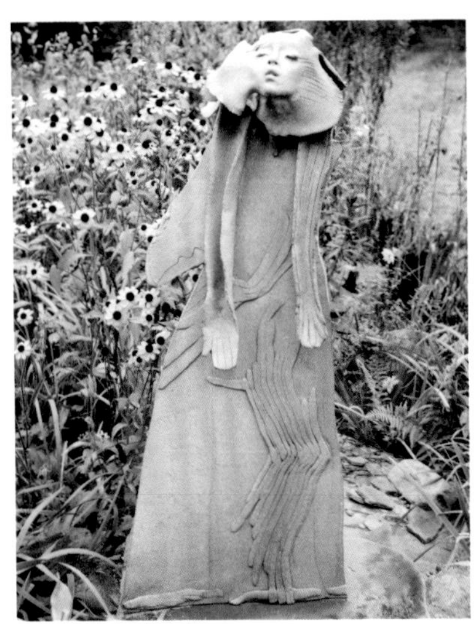

Standing Woman
1980
ceramic
37 x 12 x 15 inches

disembodied god, indwells the sinuosities and cavities in the potent comprehensive form of Mary Frank's work. He shows his presence in the physiognomies of her creations. Remaining bodiless himself, he suffuses their being, while, by the touch of her hand, Mary Frank infuses her being into the form that she creates. Mary Frank's clay sculptures are icons of touch. Some of the sculptures are large (**Horse and Rider**, 1982; **Persephone**, 1985); others though small are monumental by structure and proportions.

The artist frequently marks the surface of her sculpture with tatoo-like scratches or with the impressions of leaves and ferns in particular, or with single miniature reliefs. These are vestiges of memories of nature's verdant ground or signatures from history of times past.

In several works, movement of the body in action and movement with the wind as it blows the garments against the body are the counter players to the mind that moves within the delicate facial structure of the figures.

In the sculpture of **Standing Woman** (1980) the wind has subsided. The figure standing straight is shrouded in a stiff plank-like robe encrusted with a bold zigzag design over which hang arms that appear to be both lifeless and self-offering and resemble fringes of shawl slung around the figure's neck. A broad, striated frill, a halo, surrounds the noble head. Its full thirsty lips are parted. Unseeing eyes wait in a face made immaculate by suffering. The face is tilted at an angle in which flowers receive the light of the sun.

Hybrids and nameless creatures come to life in Mary Frank's art. In their spontaneity they have greater immediacy than the monsters fraught with symbolic meaning of ancient civilizations. There the leogryphs, centaurs and other imaginary beings are part of established myths. In Mary Frank's work nameless shapes are caught in "statu nascendi," while they are born and acquire their shape. They are near to their source, they are undefinable and unpredictable in their magical reality. They are polymorphous, polyvalent and self-explanatory; they are primary sculptural form.

The little dream horse in **Utterance** (1984), on its endless journey into the unknown, is one of the recurrent themes for more than a decade in several of Mary Frank's sculptures. It is the antithesis of a nightmare's cumbrous, oppressive, looming assault. It is a symbol of the desire for freedom, a departure from the limited self on an uncharted road. A similar horse prances along the widely extended arm of the **Woman with Small Horse** (1983). Indeed the horse seems to prance slowly and with calm assurance away from the large and noble figure of the woman, whose head, tilted in a mood of faraway detachment seems to ignore the little horse on its journey into a faraway land. A wind has come that brushes back the woman's headgear and tosses her robe all around her full figure transfixed in its own stillness. The structure of this sculpture is akin to that of the **Dream of China** (1971). The rectangularity of forearm and palm of the earlier image is suggested here by the exposed, prismatic vertical support of the sculpture and the outstretched, overlong arm. It has no hand, nothing to mark its end, for it is the road that the little horse is taking.

Mary Frank's sculptures are creations out of inner experience on several levels of consciousness. Precipitated from within, they acquire form by means of concrete elements: the inert clod of earth; the water that renders it malleable; the fire that will bake it into hardness and make durable the cavities and voids that answer the swell of its modelled and molded shapes. Modelling lays bare the sensitivity imparted to the mass. Its "nerves" are as if laid bare at the edges of form, which are sharp and cutting, tremulous or flowing, rough or smooth. The expressiveness of the edge surpasses that of the line because the edge carries with it the quality of the mass, the ponderosity that terminates as edge.

Frenzy inhabits **Horse and Rider** (1982). Mountains crouch and sink, self-consuming towards the abyss below the racing horse which is wildly straining forward, outdistancing itself, ahead of itself by one head, and which, in fact, has become two heads snorting the fire of speed from dark pits of nostrils, mouth and eyes. The horse's jaws quiver lest the fire consume them. Two-headed, its breath is the wind that generates and propels the paddles of their never seen before physiognomy. While the horse outdistances itself, its body cleaves; the rider gropes for a hold above the fiery abyss; a pad swatted onto his arm arrests his groping hand on the long stretch of the horse's neck. The rider is a tortured figure holding on to itself in futile terror that dilates his face, which is raised away from the chasm below and limitless void above. The stern right angle of his dwindling raised arm cuts into it. The racing horse flees under that stern angle and the twitching hand on its neck. The man's leg over the smoothly powerful horse's flank is fractured. The horse's body peels off its physicality in shards as thin as those of the mountain scenario below.

The iconography of the sculptures by Mary Frank unfolds together with their form. It is the shard in its volumetric shape, convex or concave, that is part of a whole. This whole is larger than the entire figure,

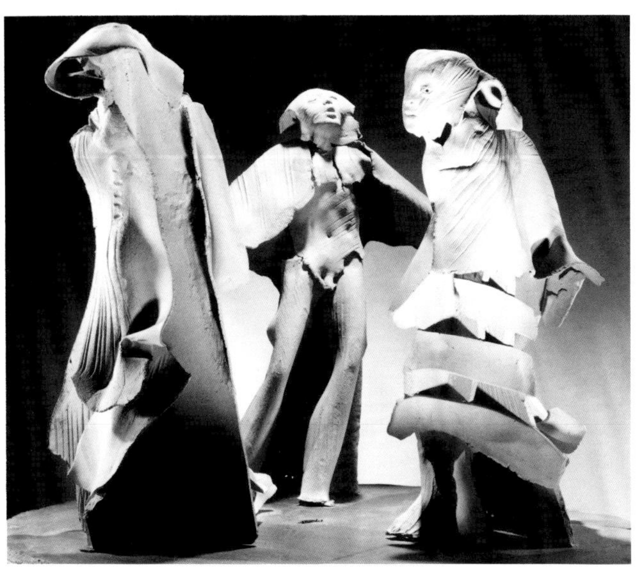

Three Dancers
1981
ceramic
25 1/2 x 34 x 25 inches

because in its unfragmented stage the interval of space is included in the form. Where another material, as for instance, plaster, is used and inventively combined with branches (**Running Man**, 1981), the running man is part of a different world of planes and solids and purposeful action. But even where clay is the material (**Three Dancers**, 1981), the several shards are placed as planes defining or enveloping a spatial core, or setting off modelled shapes. The power of the broken shard generates a spatial context of volumetric constituents. The whole of the space in between these parts, being larger than their sum, lends itself to embodying visions of apocalyptic grandeur and sensuous intensity, not to be met anywhere outside the charmed assemblage of "broken" shards.

The same degree of "unearthly" power evident in **Horse and Rider** indwells the image of **Persephone** (1985). The swell in the modelling of the human body and the transfiguring passion of the face are in tune with the soaring shapes of limbs in their nakedness and with the windswept mane of hair. This woman is not a saint, though she vies in her abandon with Bernini's "Saint Teresa." She was not created by Mary Frank with the intention of making an image of Persephone. No literary source or intermediary stood between Mary Frank and her work. As the artist herself says, "I'm not sure that she is mythological but I do know that at best working is." (*Mary Frank: Persephone Studies*, The Brooklyn Museum, 1987, exhibition catalogue).

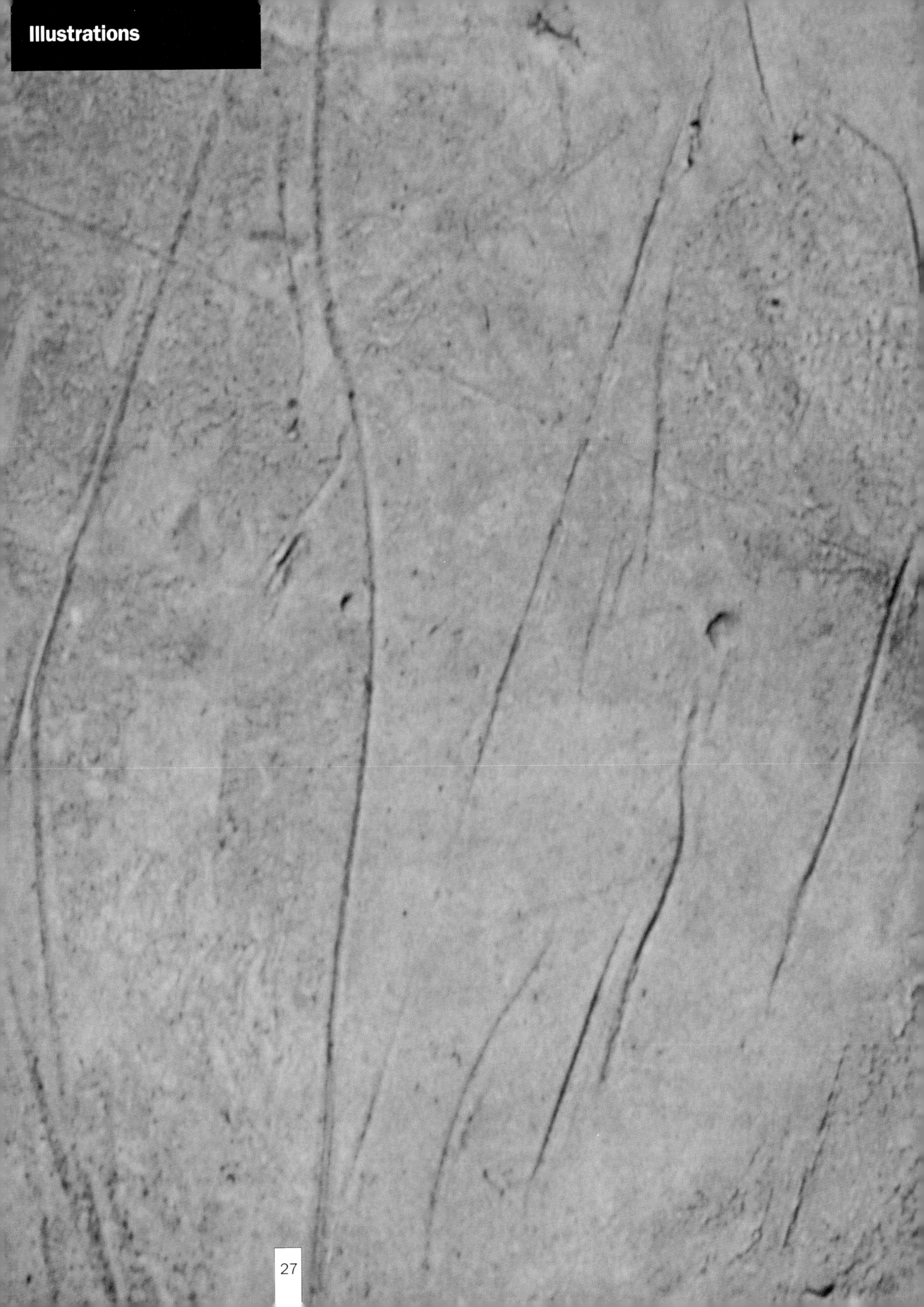

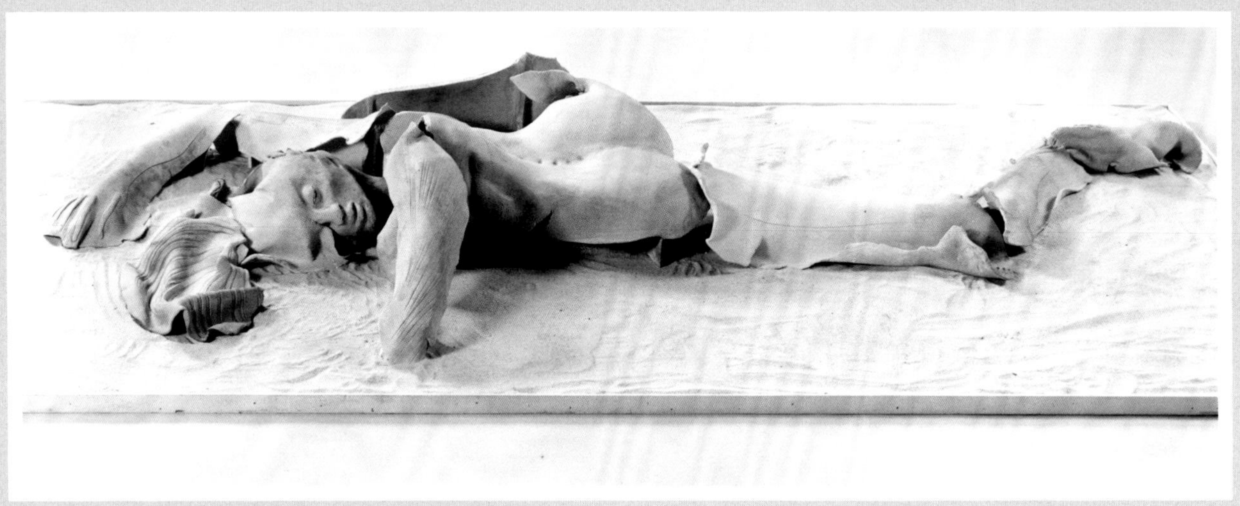

Woman Lying Down
1980
ceramic
11 3/4 x 39 x 84 inches

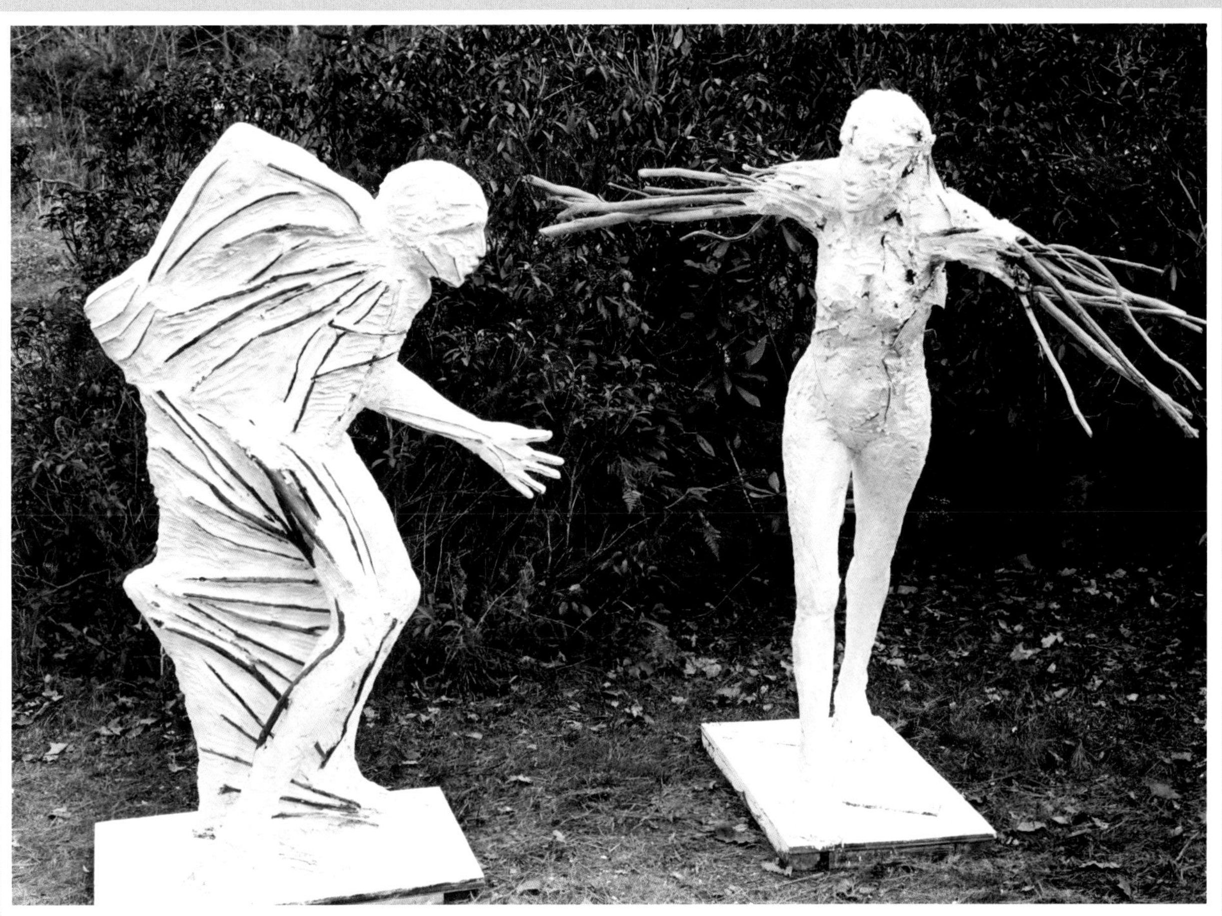

Running Man
1981
plaster and branches
63 1/2 x 25 1/2 x 45 inches

Walking Woman
1981
plaster and branches
65 x 61 x 57 inches

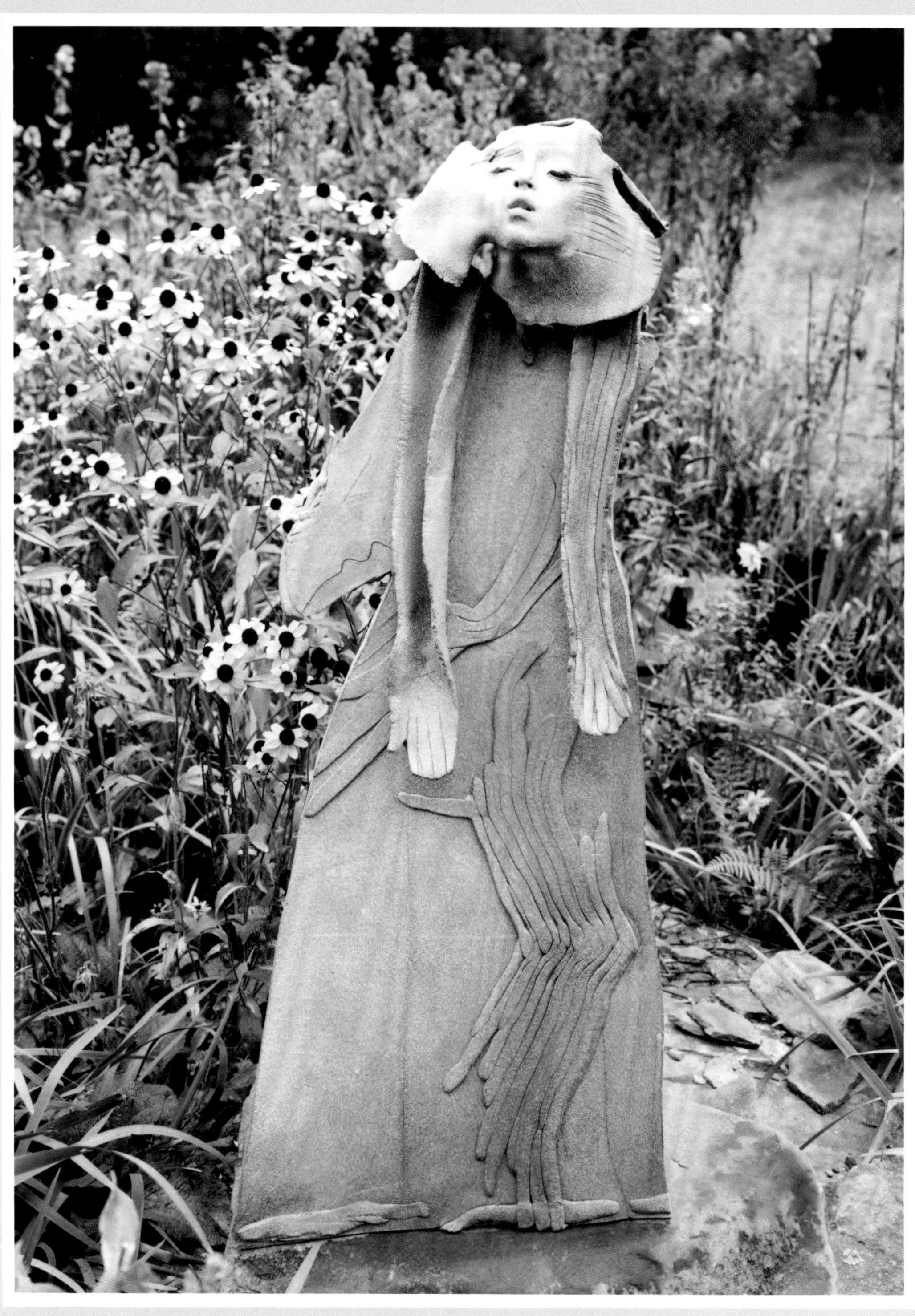

Standing Woman
1980
ceramic
37 x 12 x 15 inches

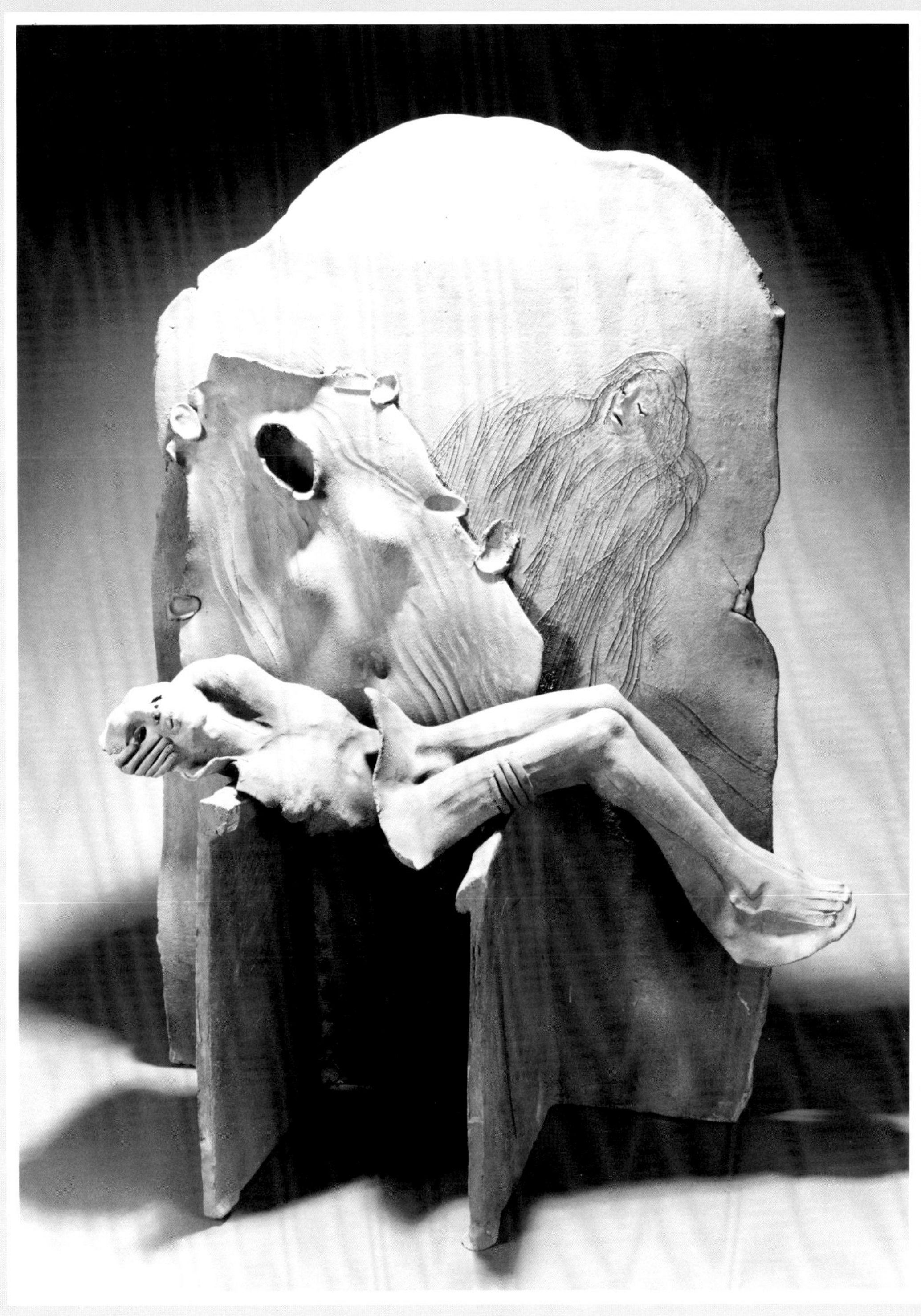

Pieta
1981
ceramic
36 3/4 x 28 1/2 x 17 inches

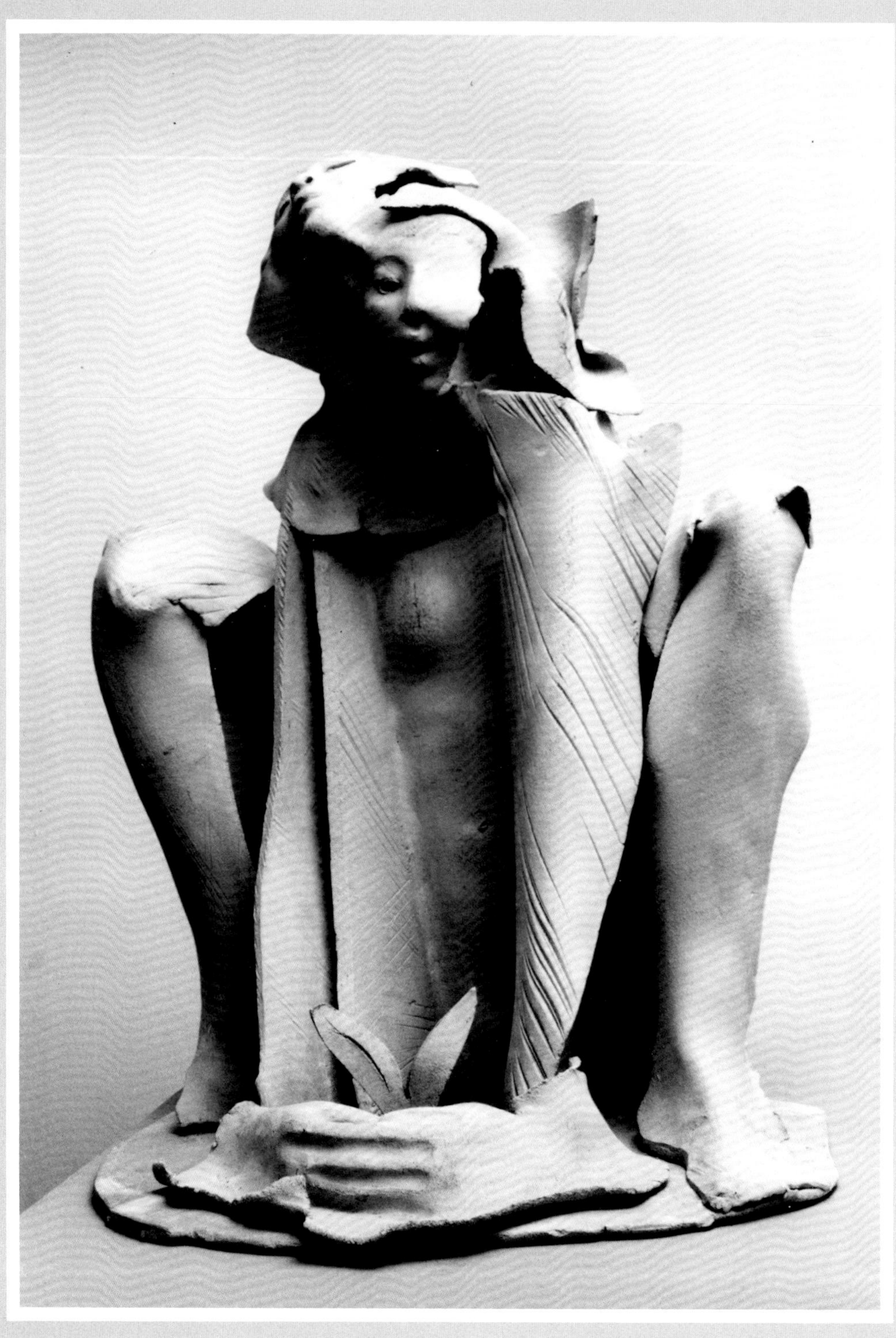

Crouching Woman with Two Faces
1981
ceramic
29 x 24 x 16 inches

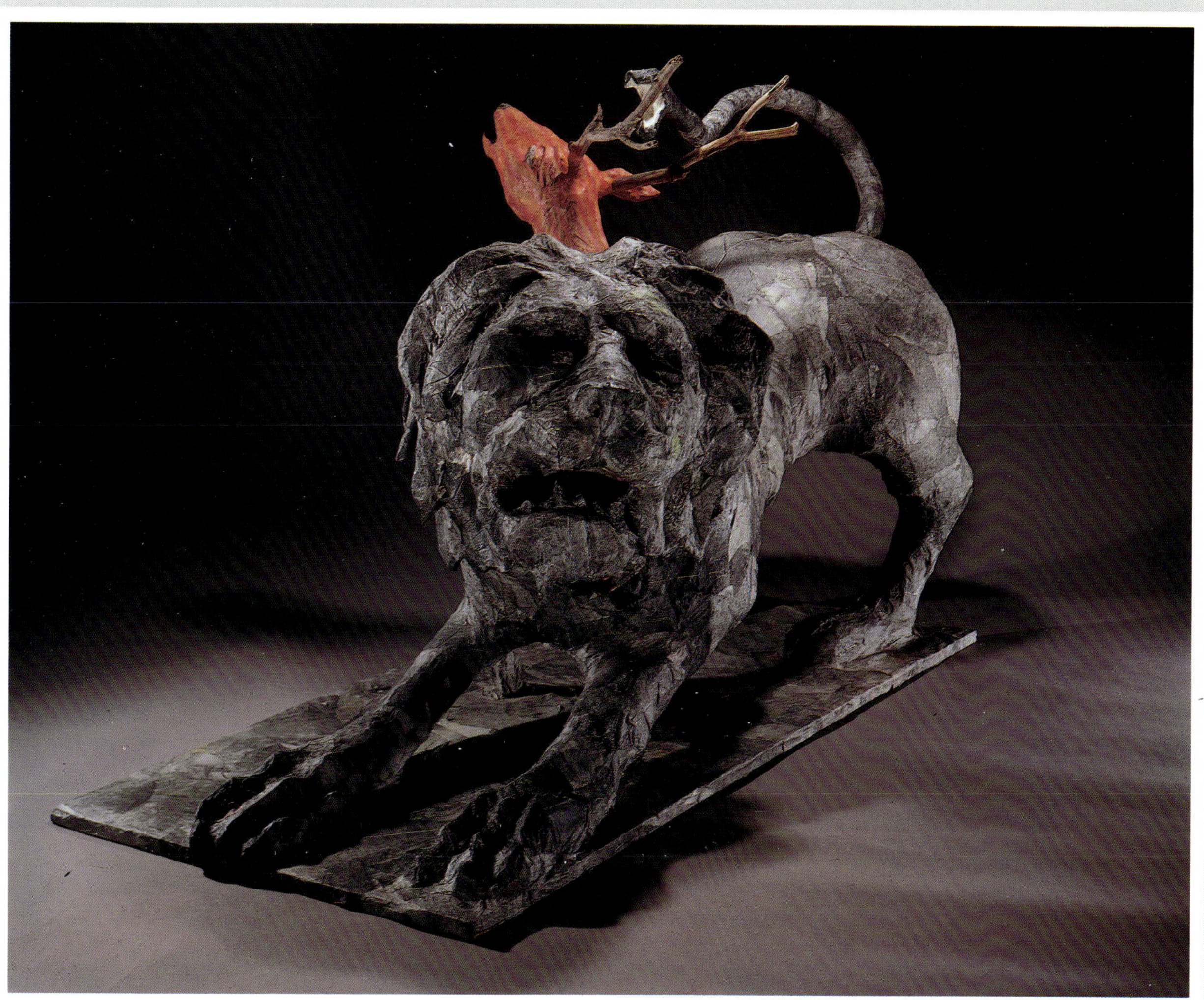

Chimera
1984-86
papier mache
34 x 60 x 24 inches

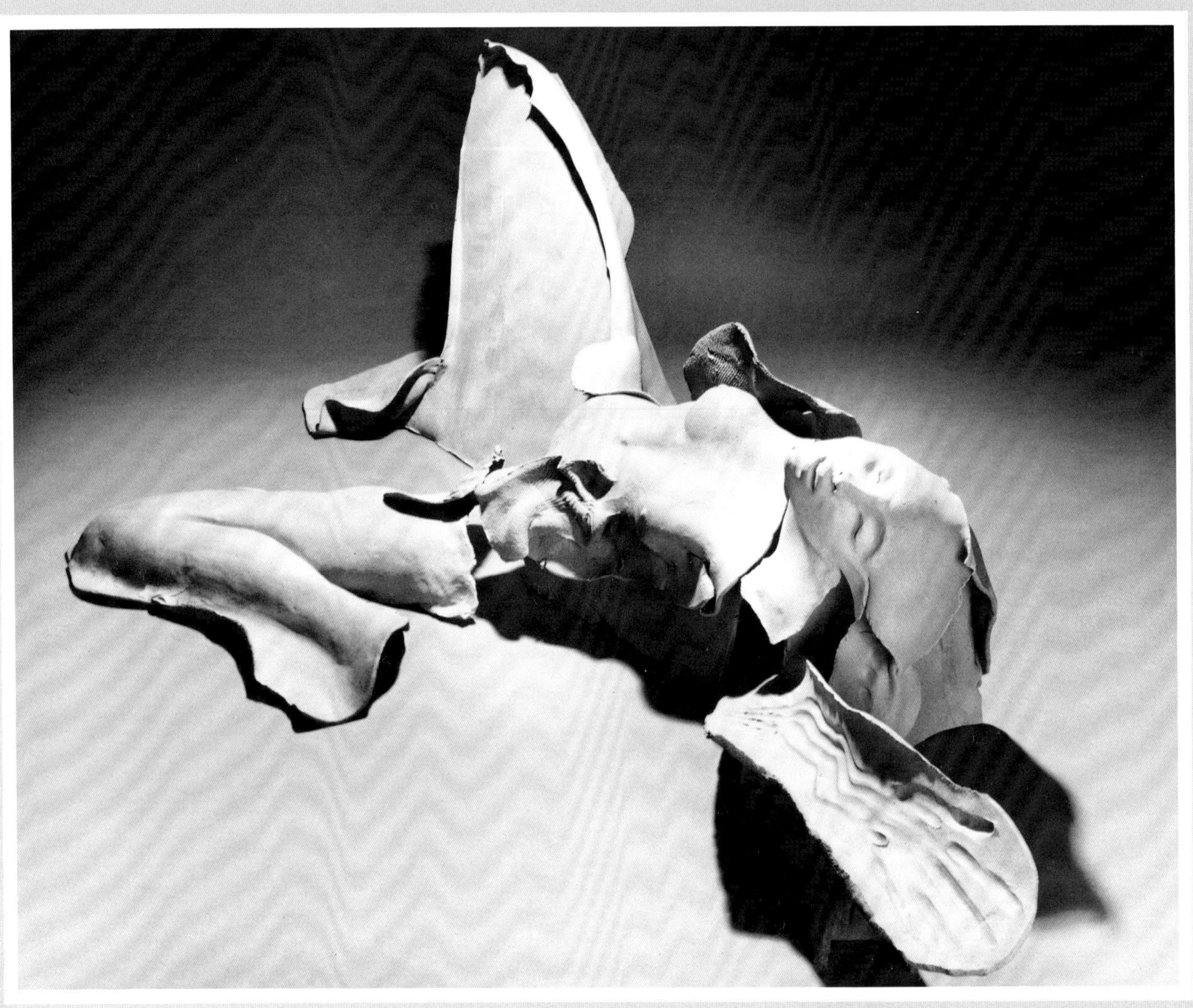

Persephone
1985
ceramic
25 x 74 x 38 inches

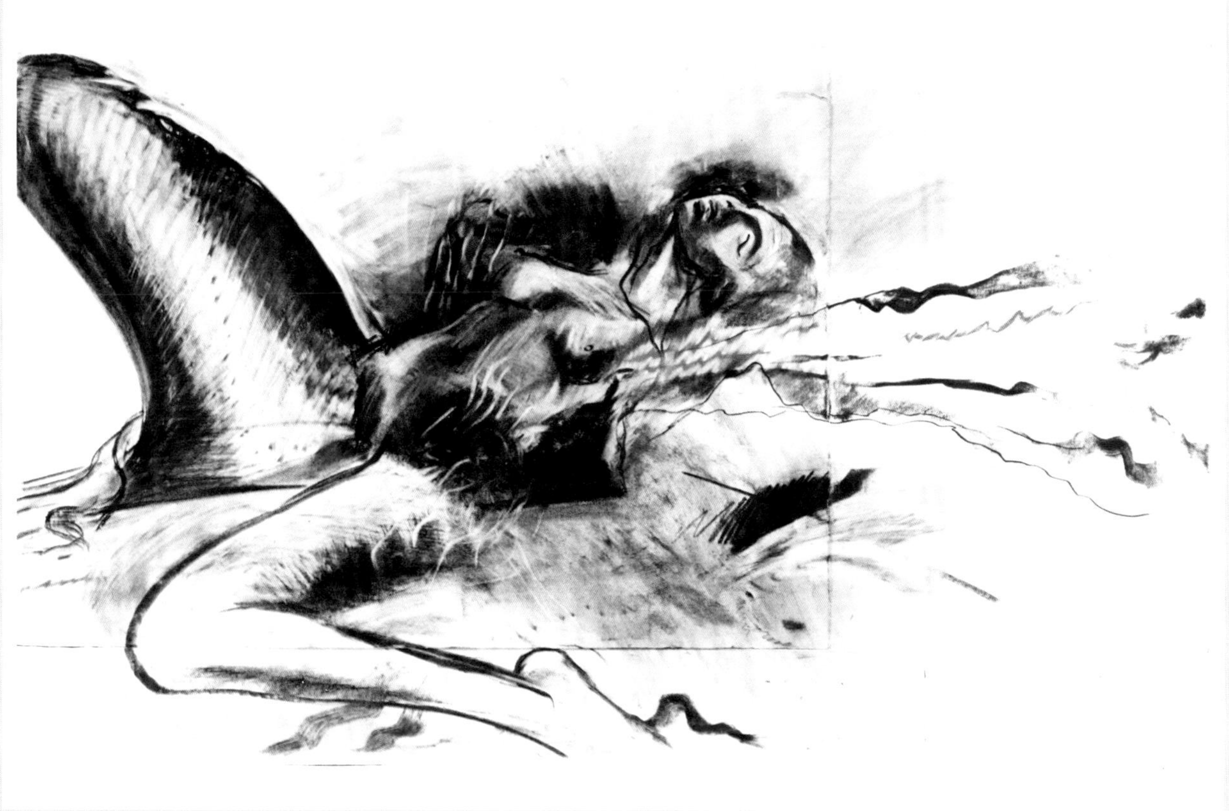

Persephone
1985
charcoal on paper
35 x 59 inches

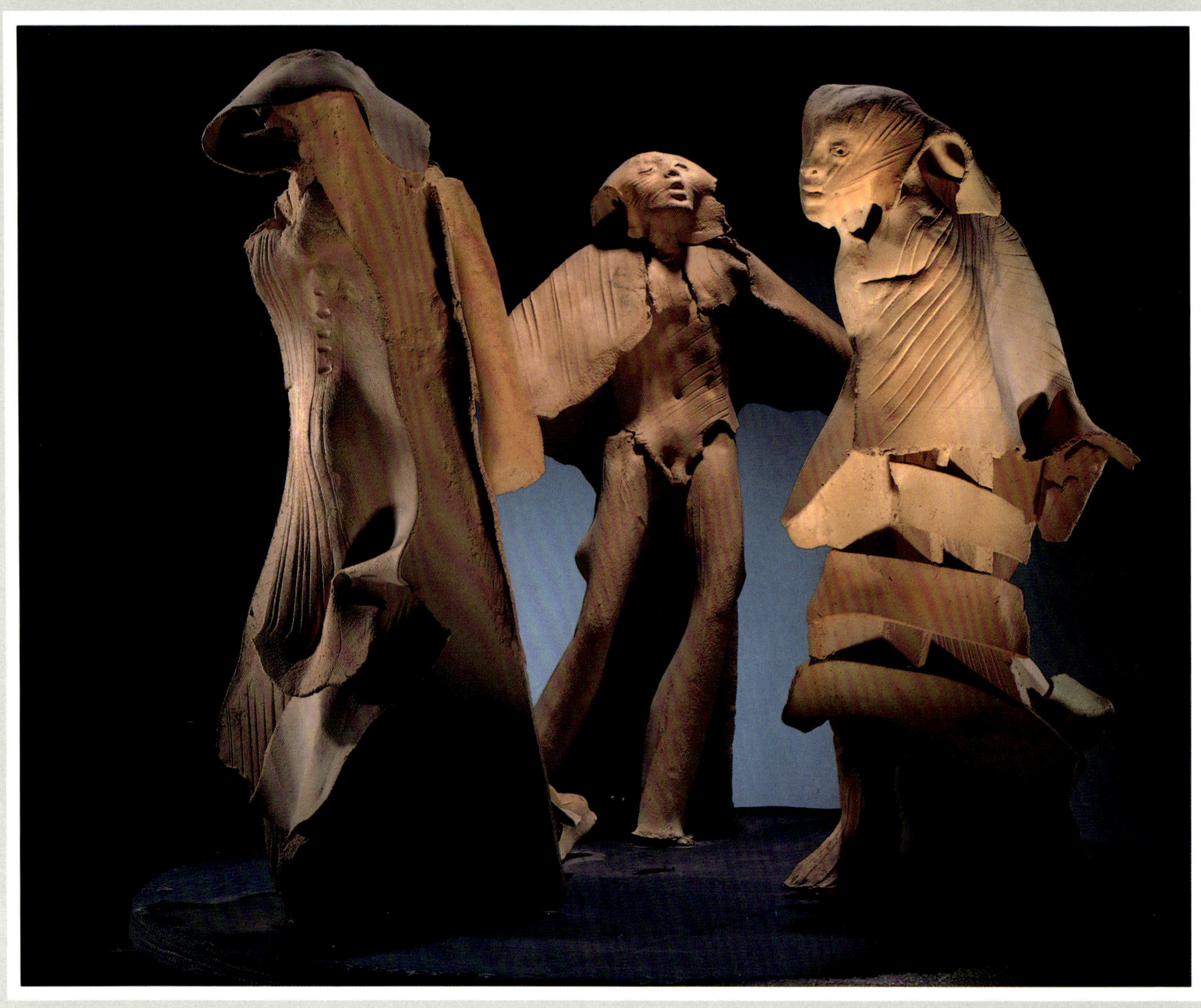

Three Dancers
1981
ceramic
25 1/2 x 34 x 25 inches

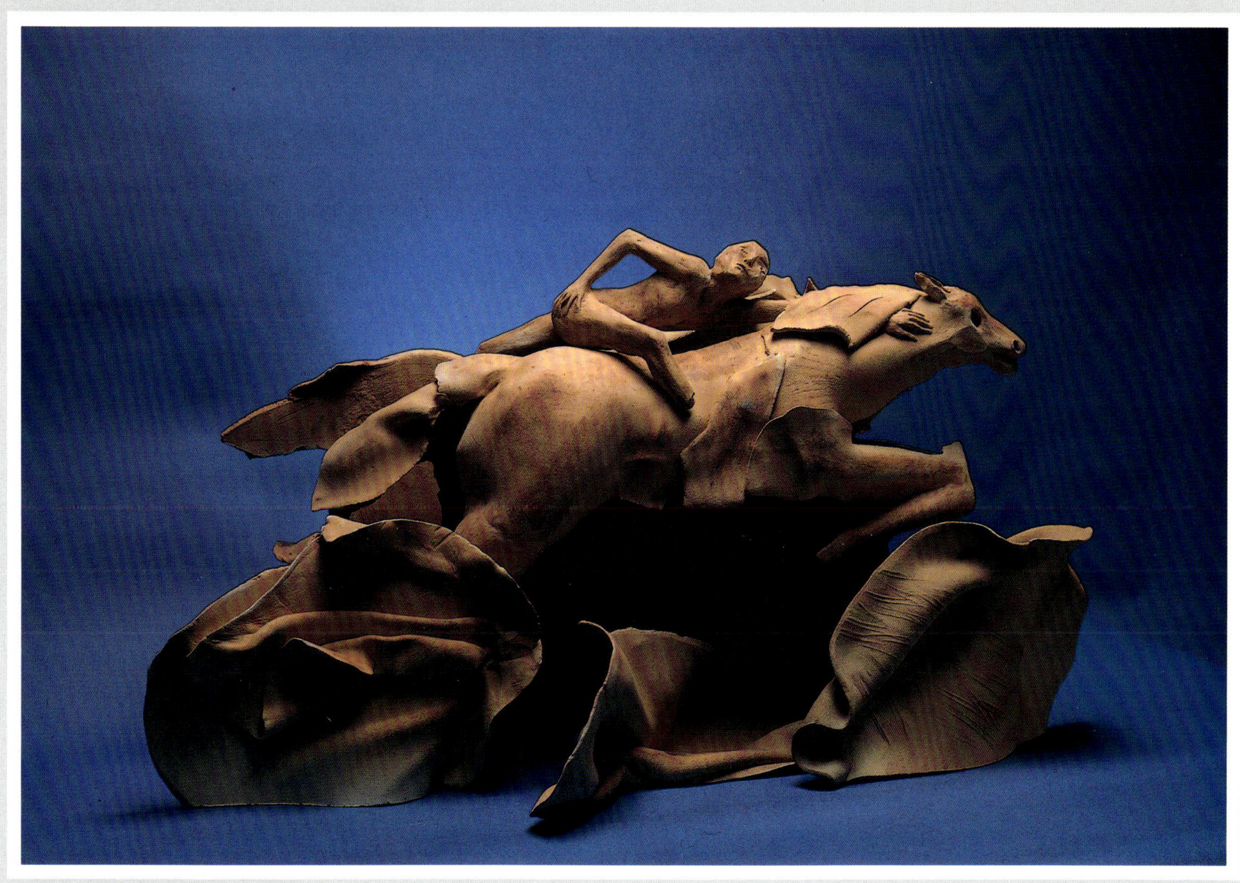

Horse and Rider
1982
ceramic
24 x 43 x 31 1/2 inches

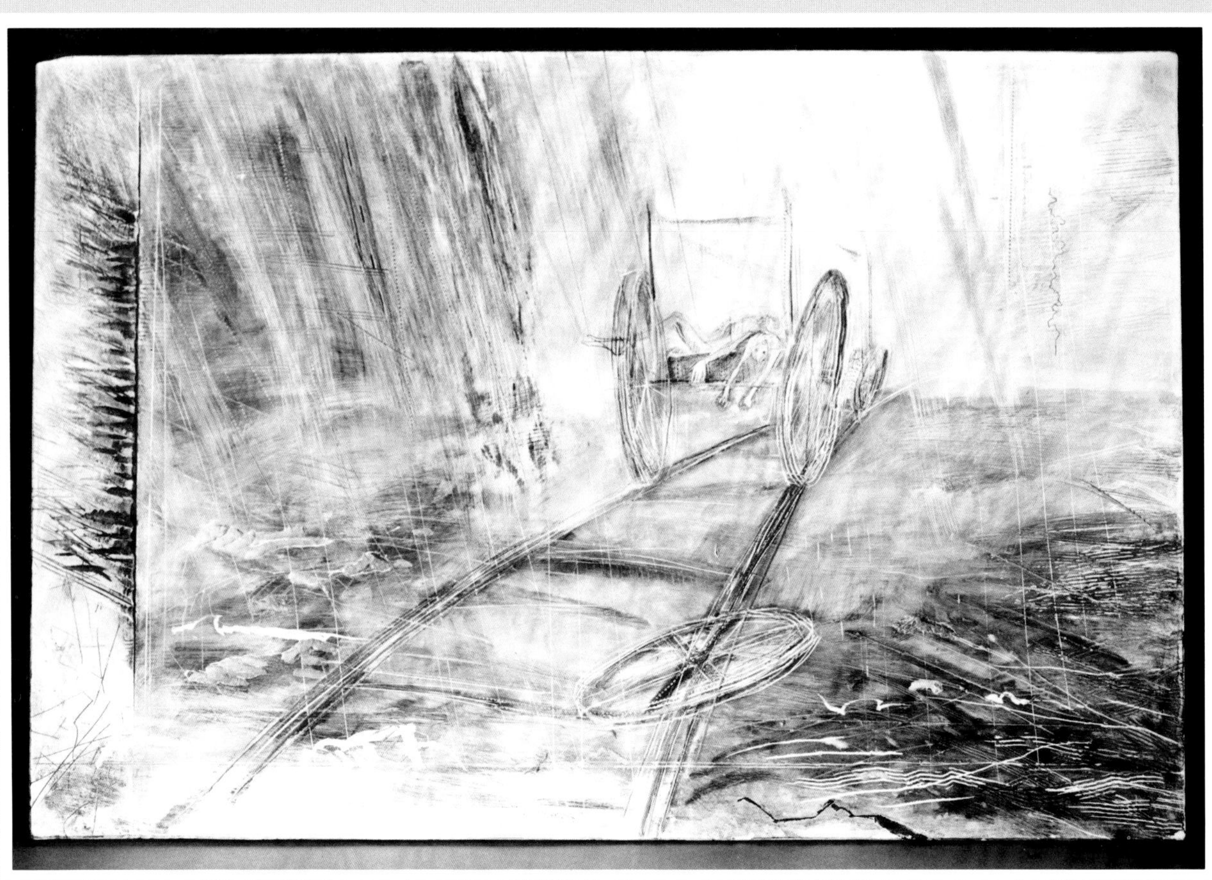

The Cart
1986
plaster, oil paint
18 1/2 x 28 inches

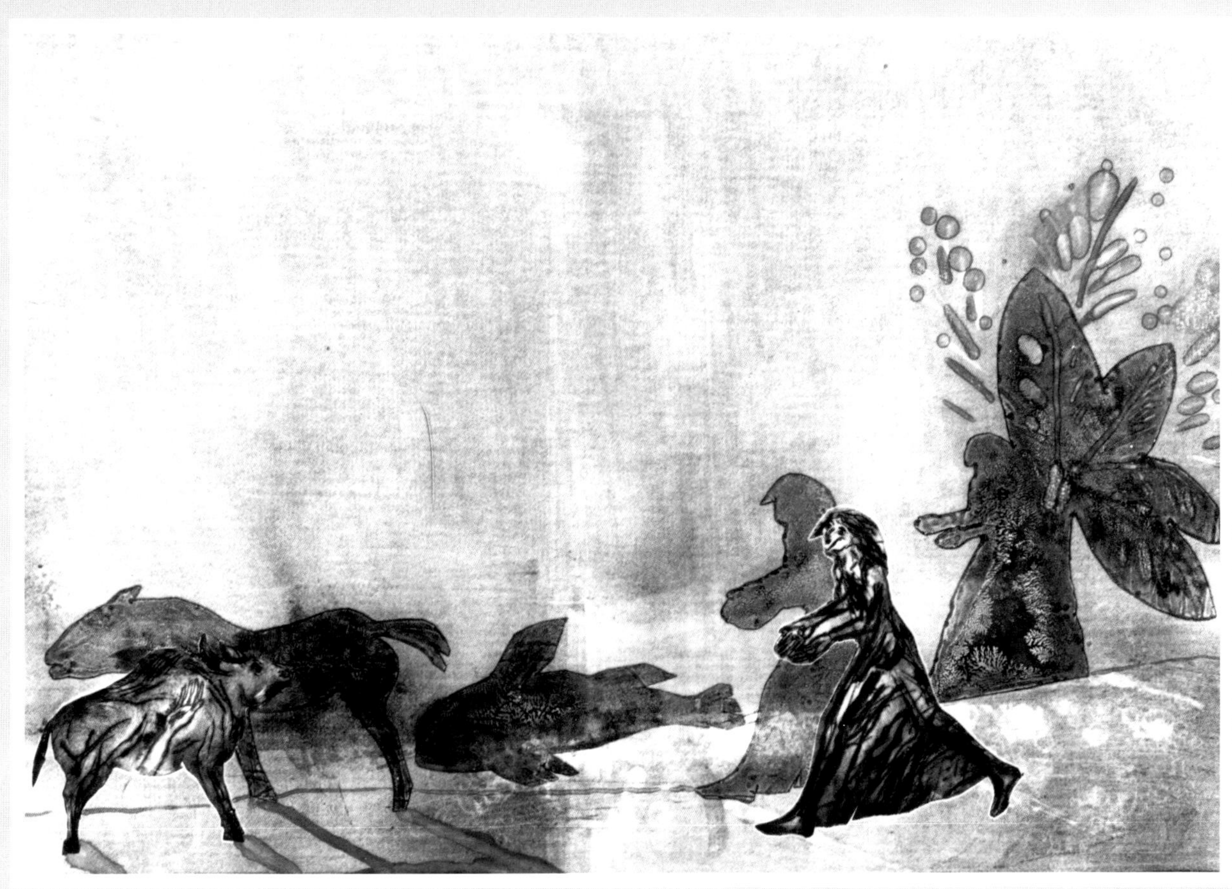

The Storm is Here
1982
monoprint and drypoint on paper
23 3/4 x 35 3/8 inches

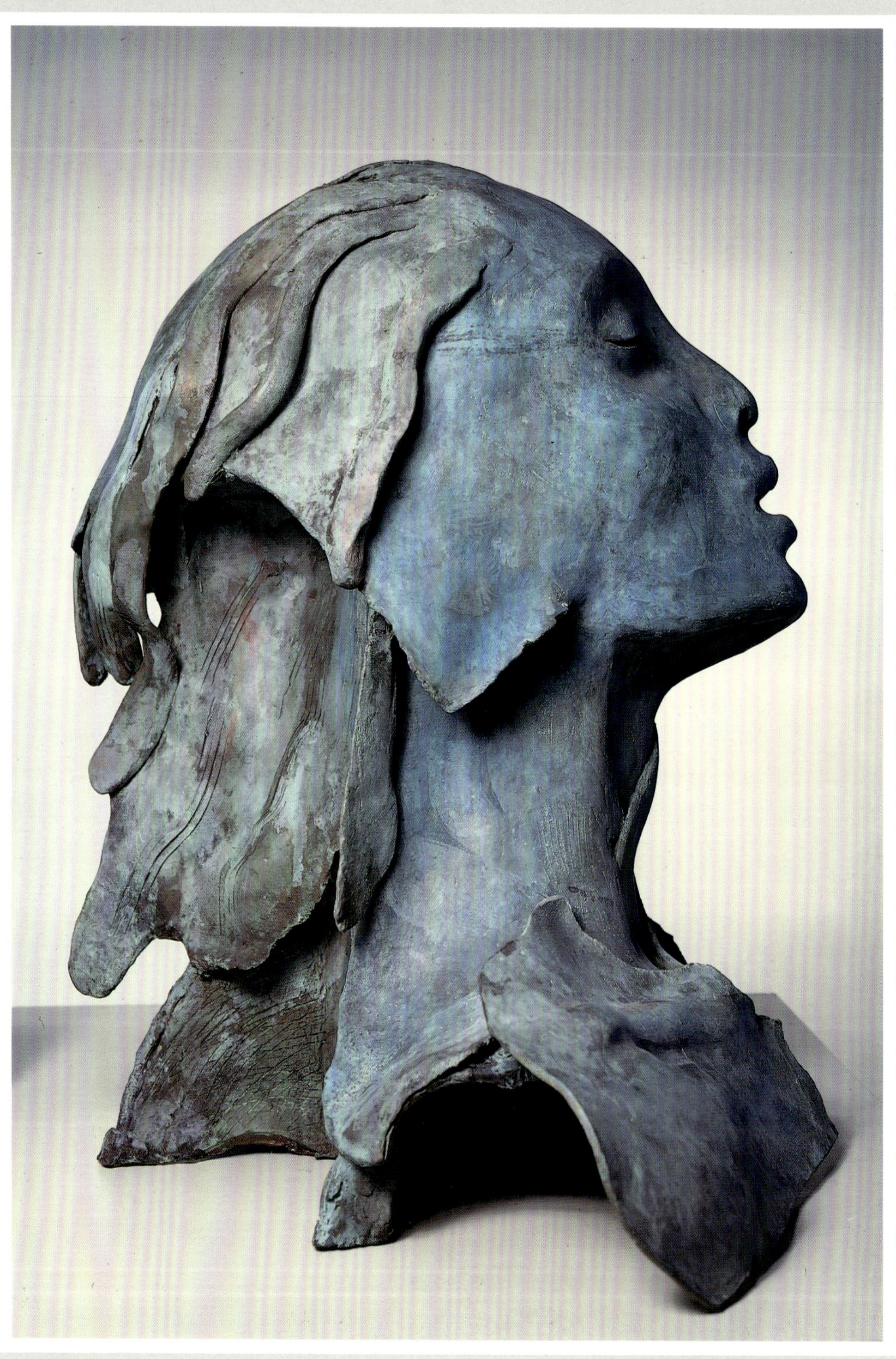

Head
1985/86
bronze
28 x 34 x 22 inches

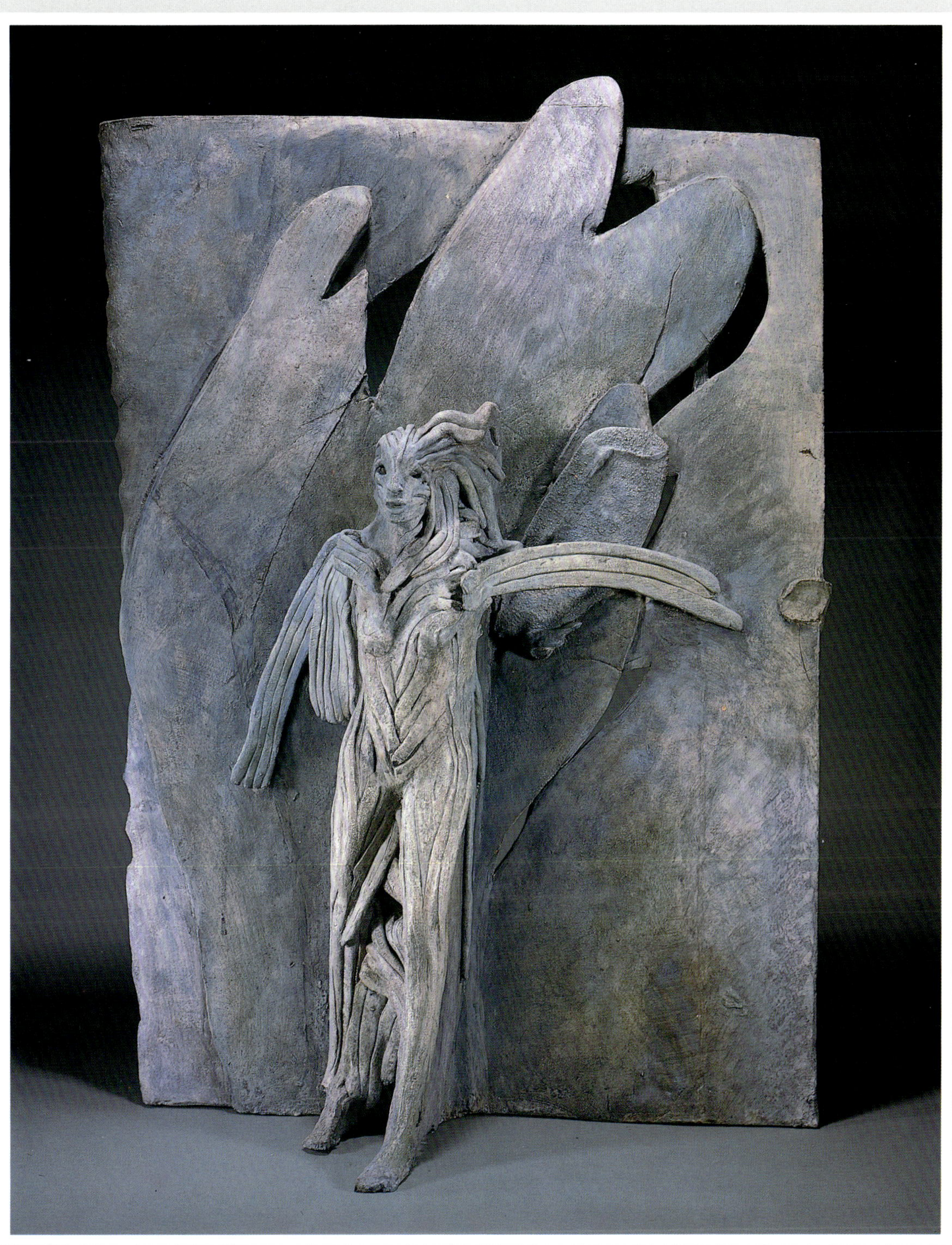

Ethiopian
1986/87
oil on ceramic
27 1/2 x 20 x 14 inches

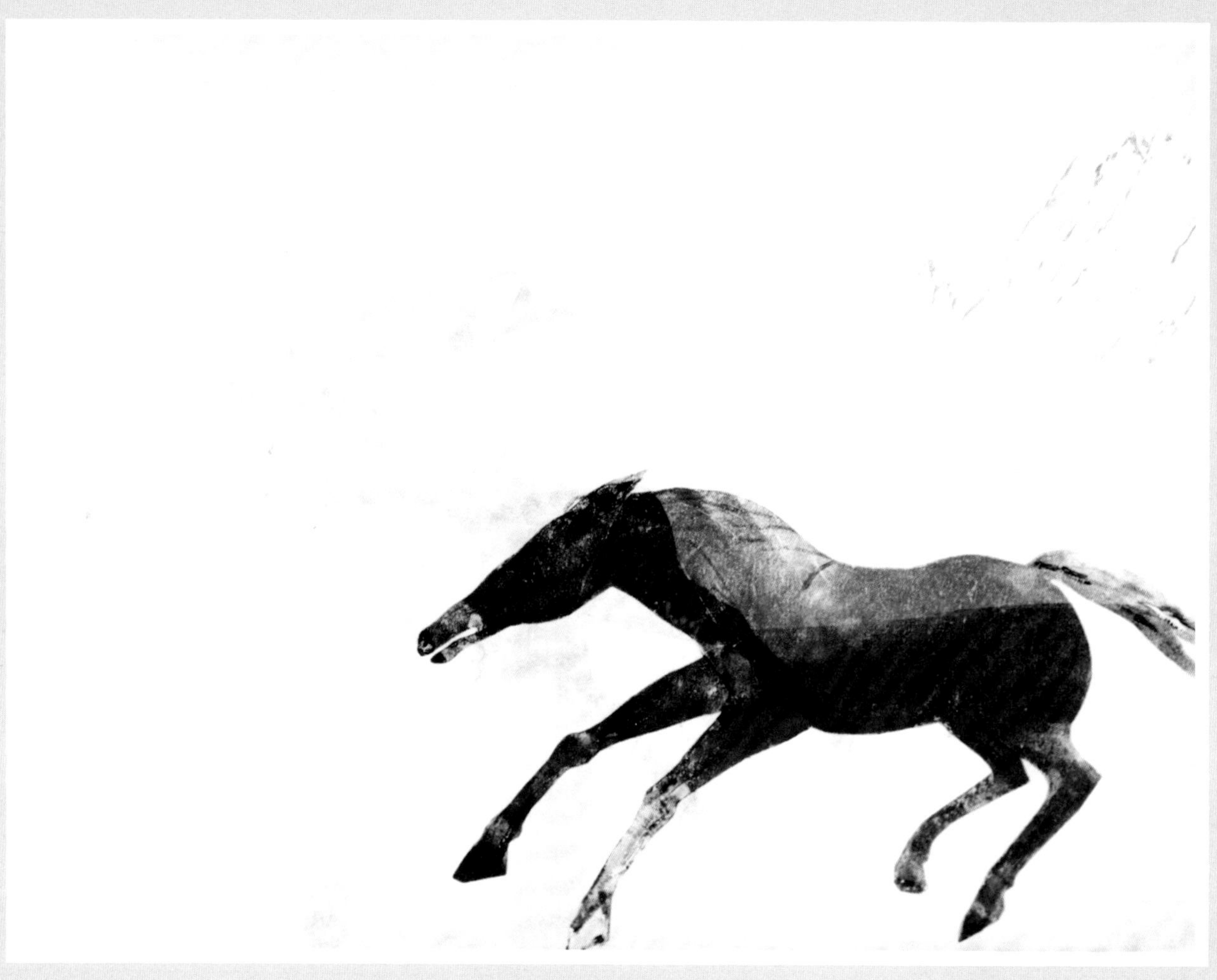

Spirit Riders
1982
monoprint on paper
29 1/2 x 40 5/8 inches

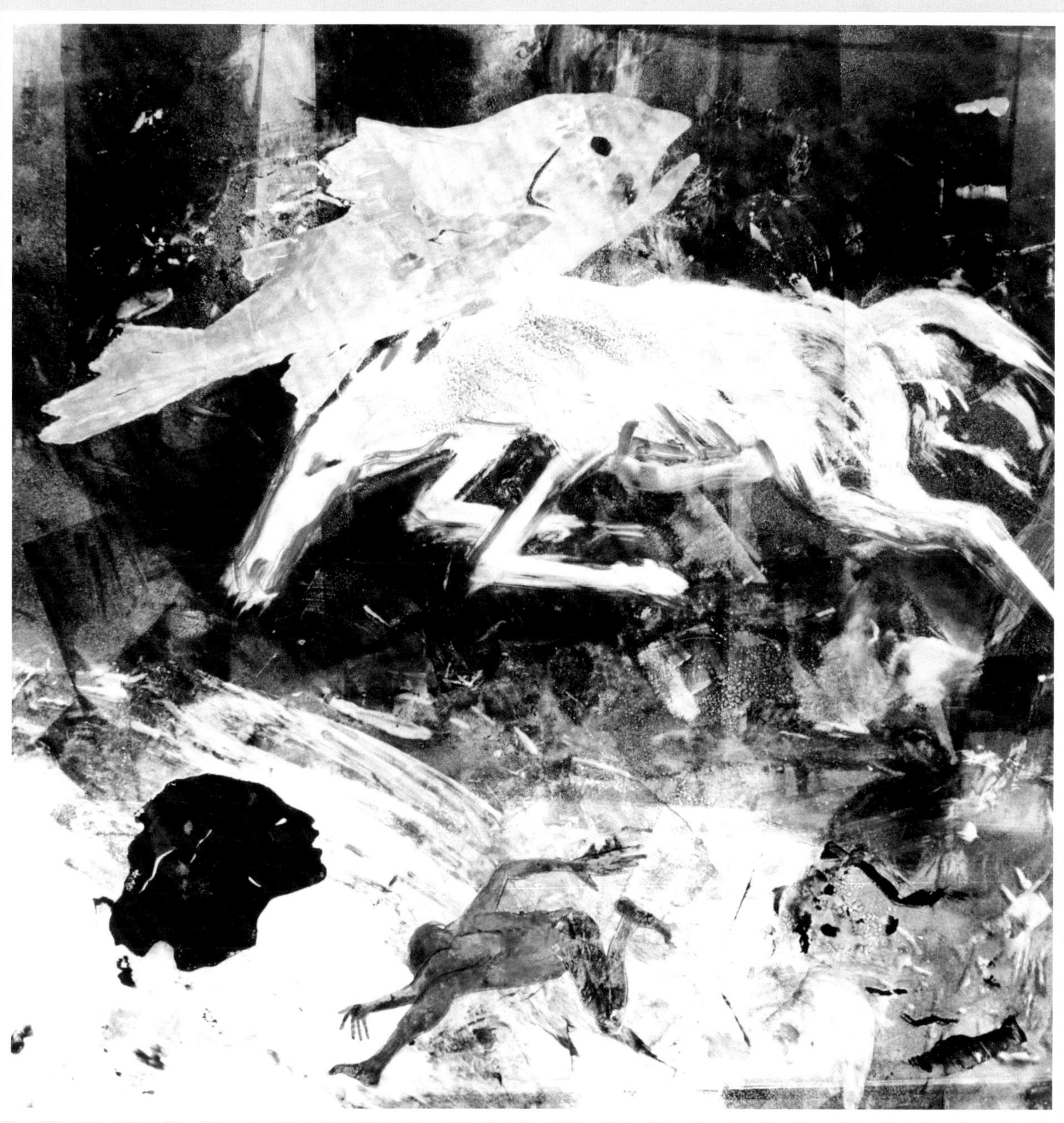

Pandemonium
1983
monoprint on paper
27 5/8 x 27 3/4 inches

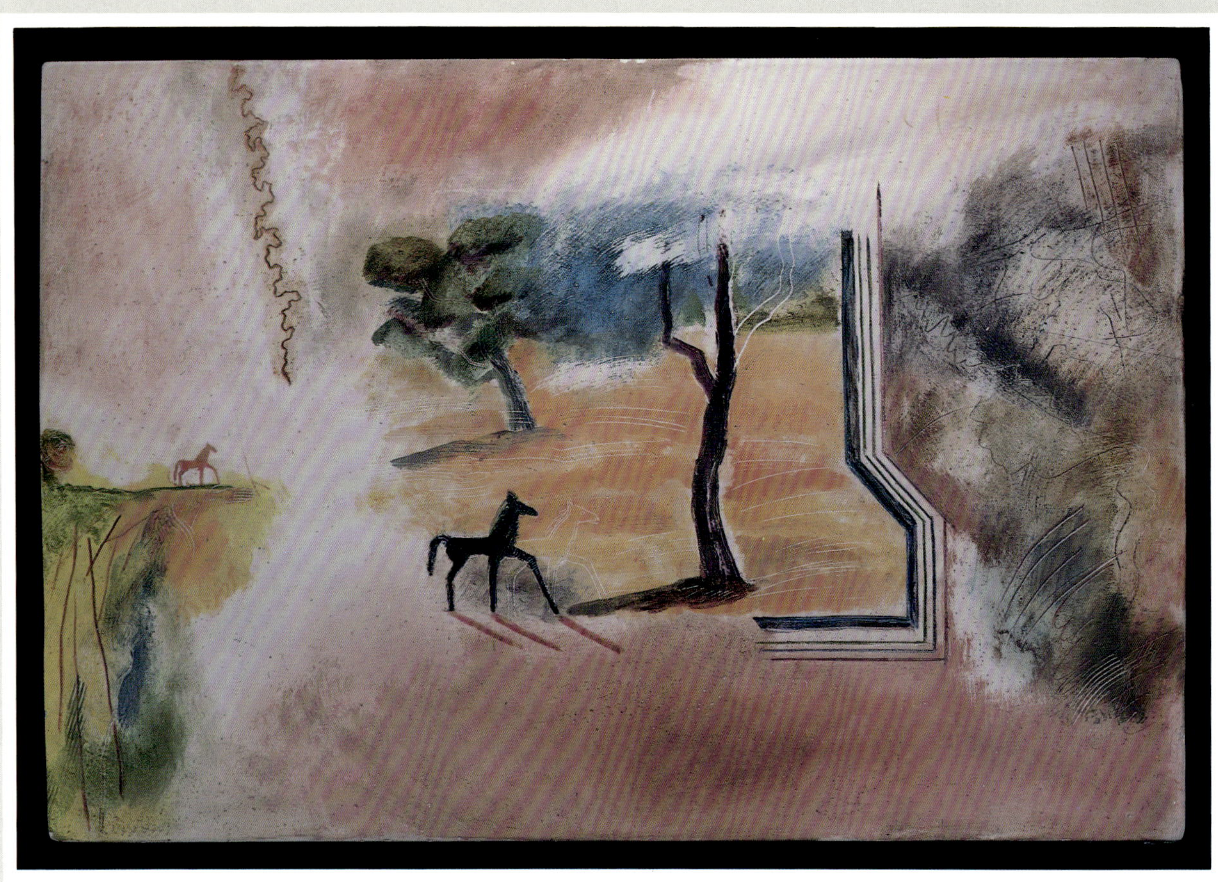

Passage
1986
plaster, oil paint
18 1/2 x 28 inches

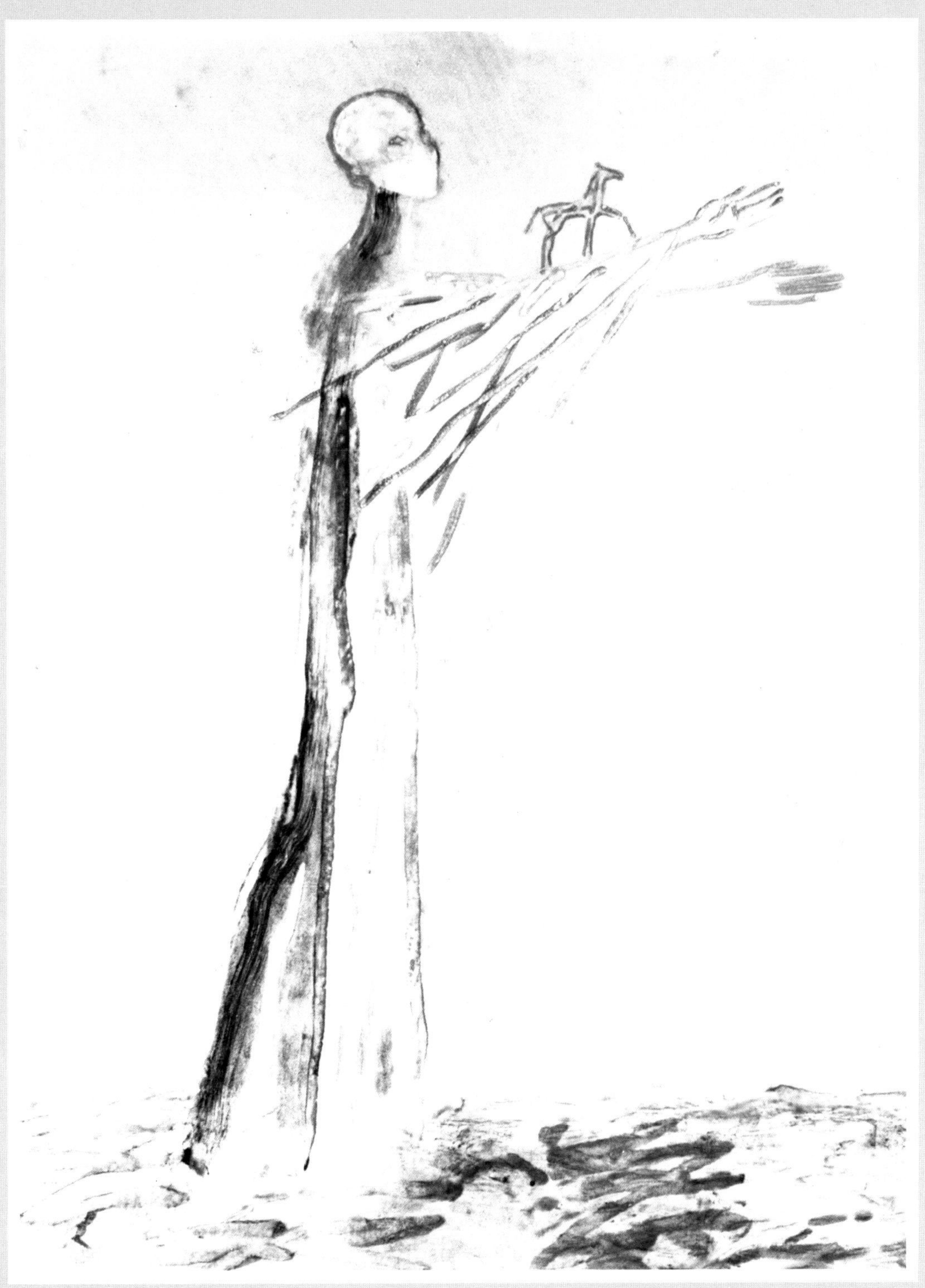

Utterance
1983
monoprint on paper
33 x 25 1/2 inches

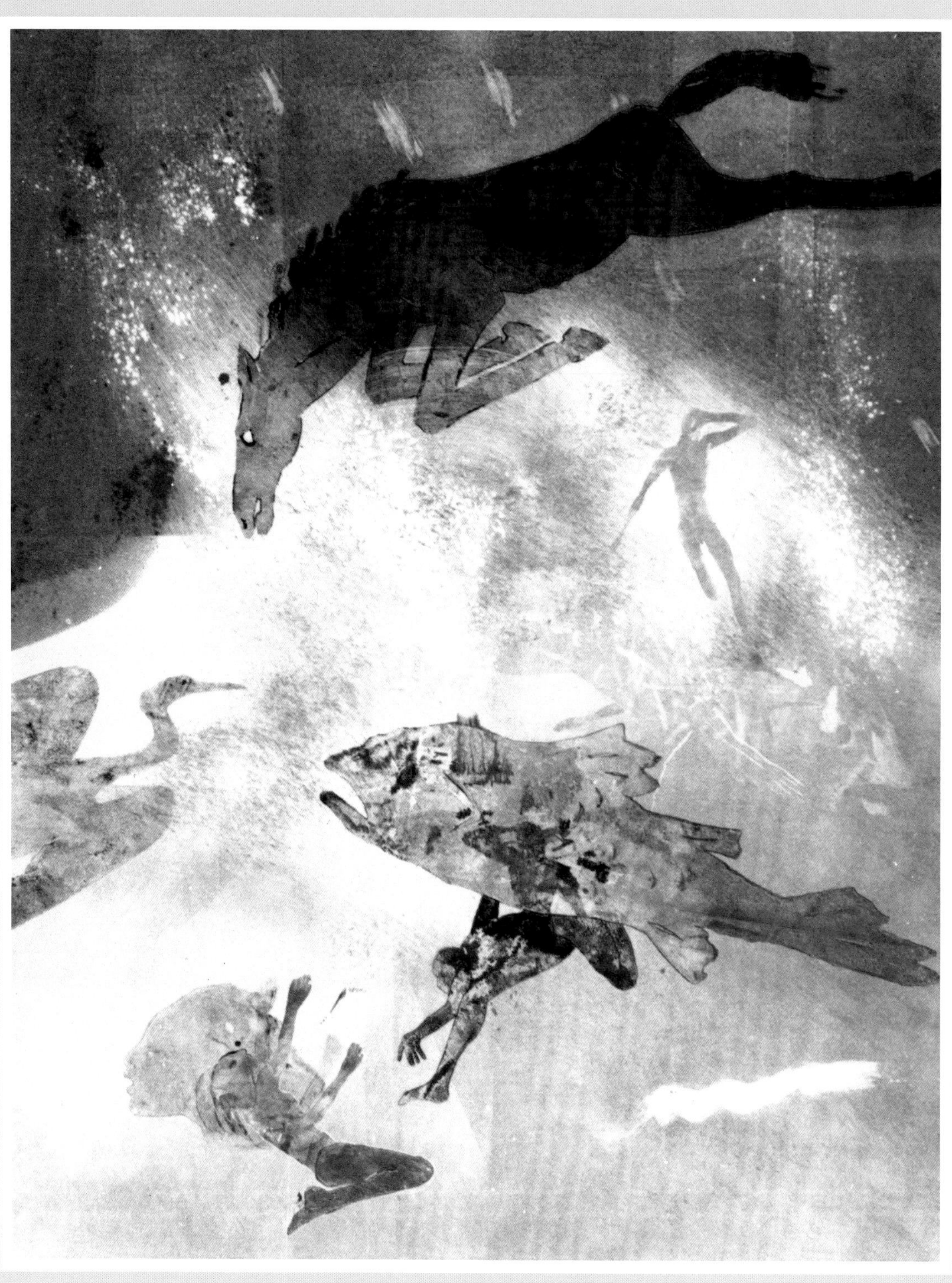

Leap
1984
monoprint on paper
36 x 27 7/8 inches

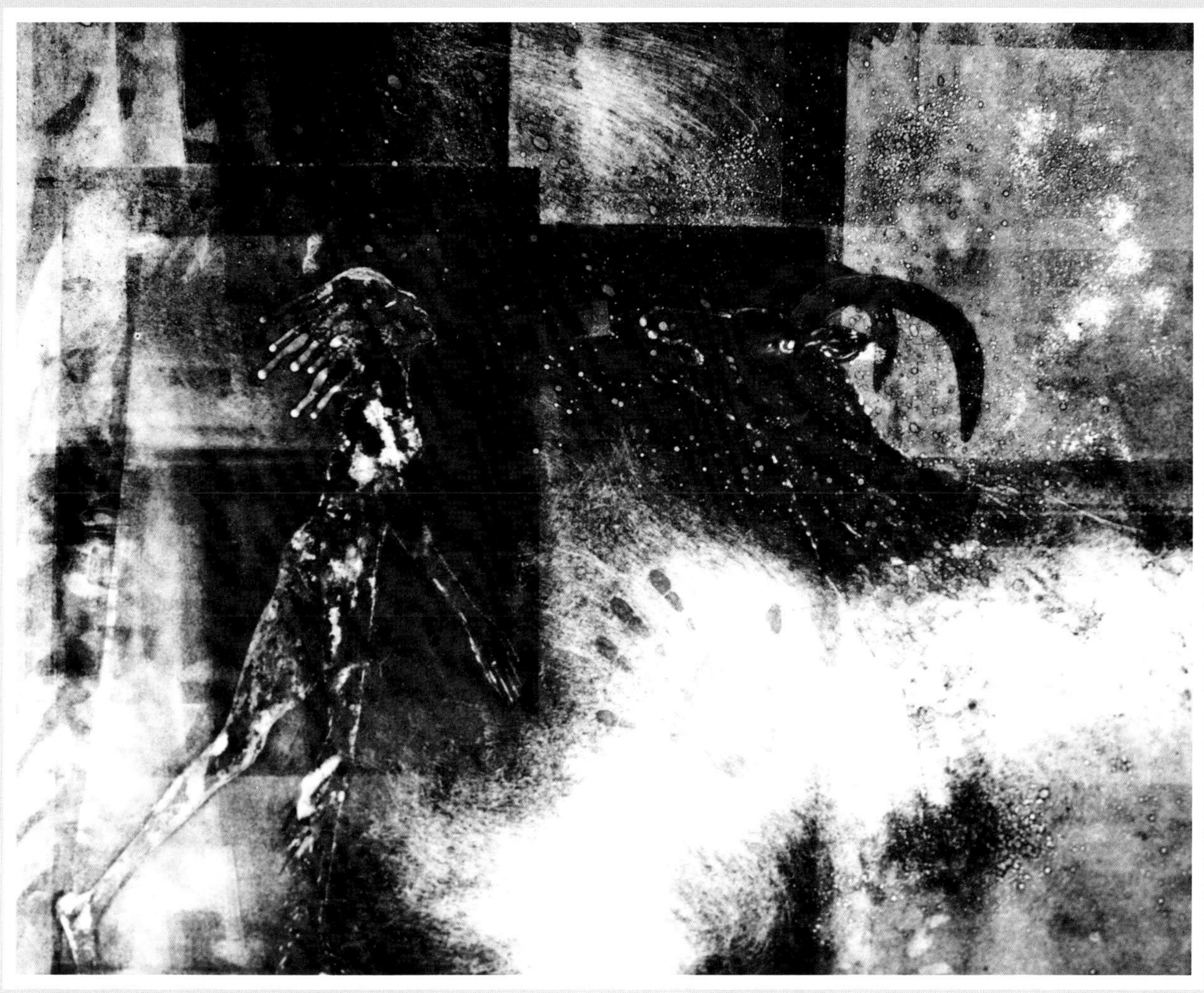

Recognition
1984
monoprint on paper
27 5/8 x 36 1/2 inches

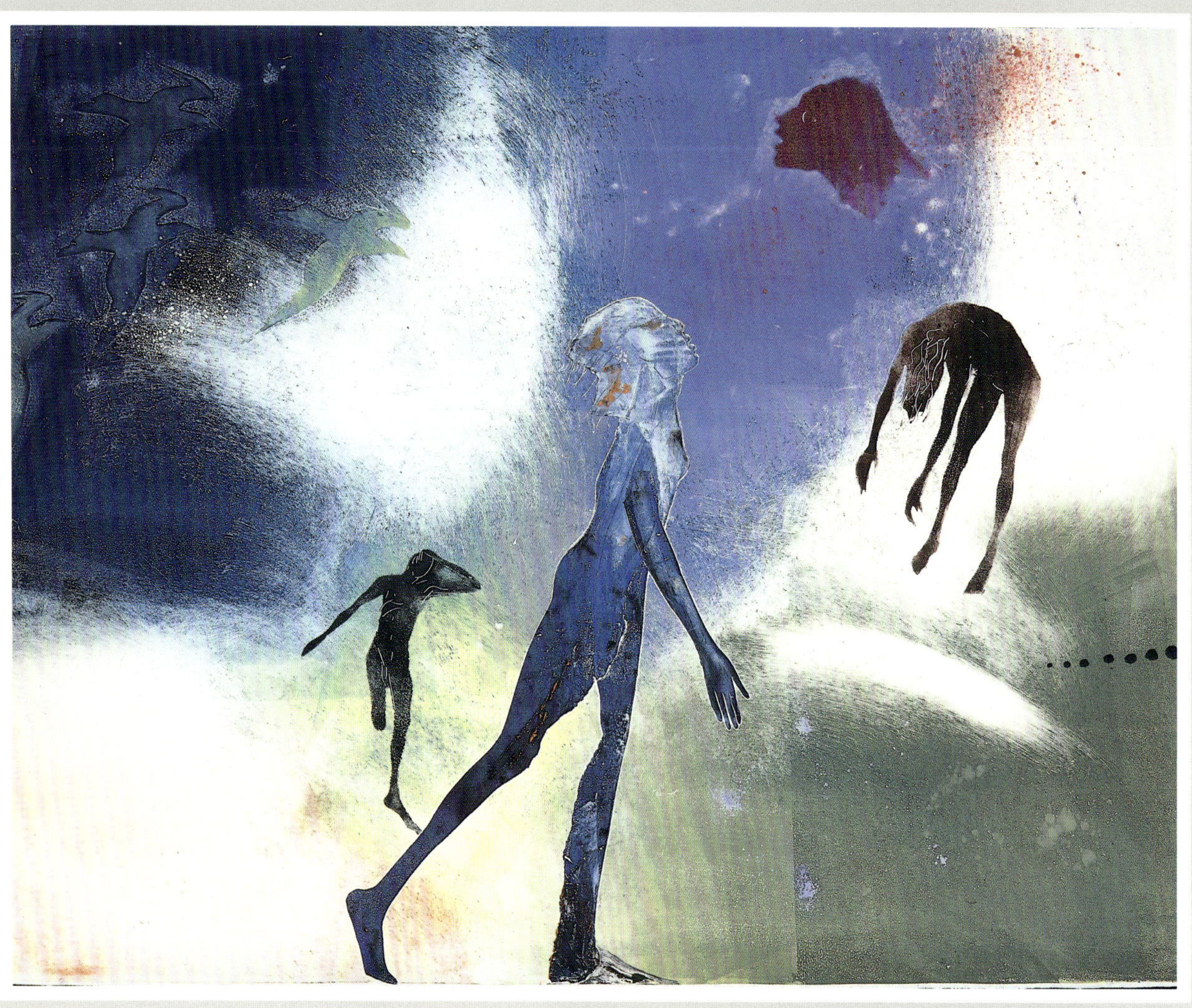

Suspension
1984
monoprint on paper
27 7/8 x 35 7/8 inches

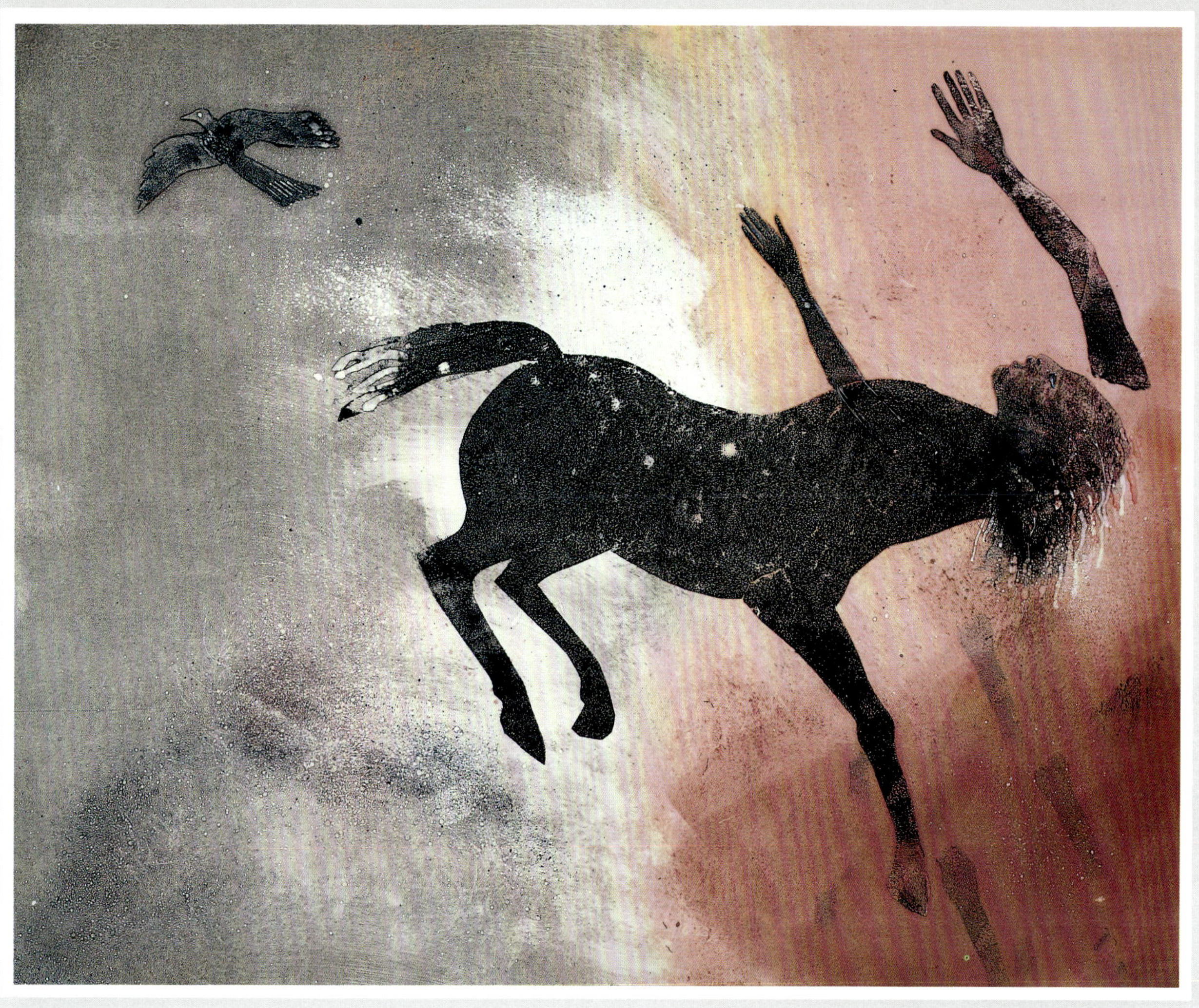

Centaur
1984
monoprint on paper
27 7/8 x 35 7/8 inches

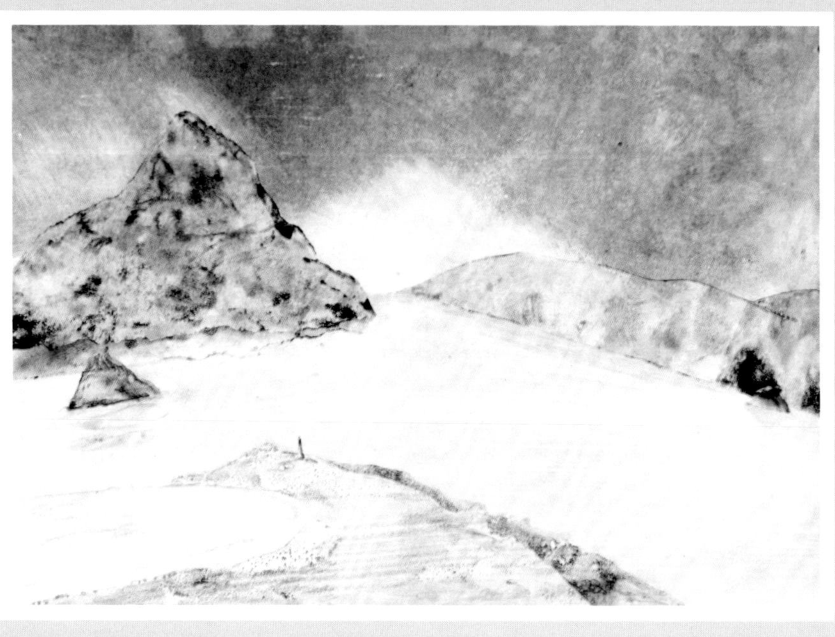

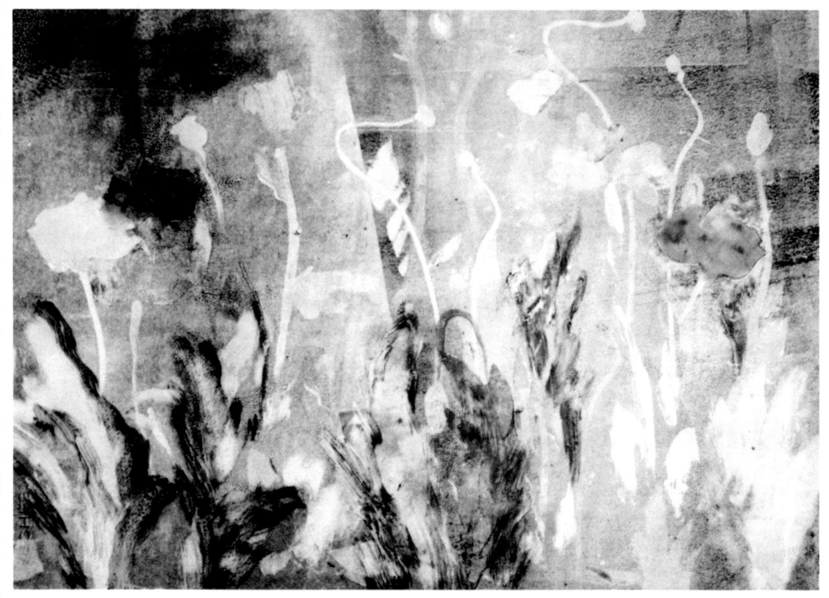

At the Edge
1984
monoprint on rice paper
25 1/4 x 38 3/4 inches

Poppies
1979
monoprint on paper
26 x 38 inches

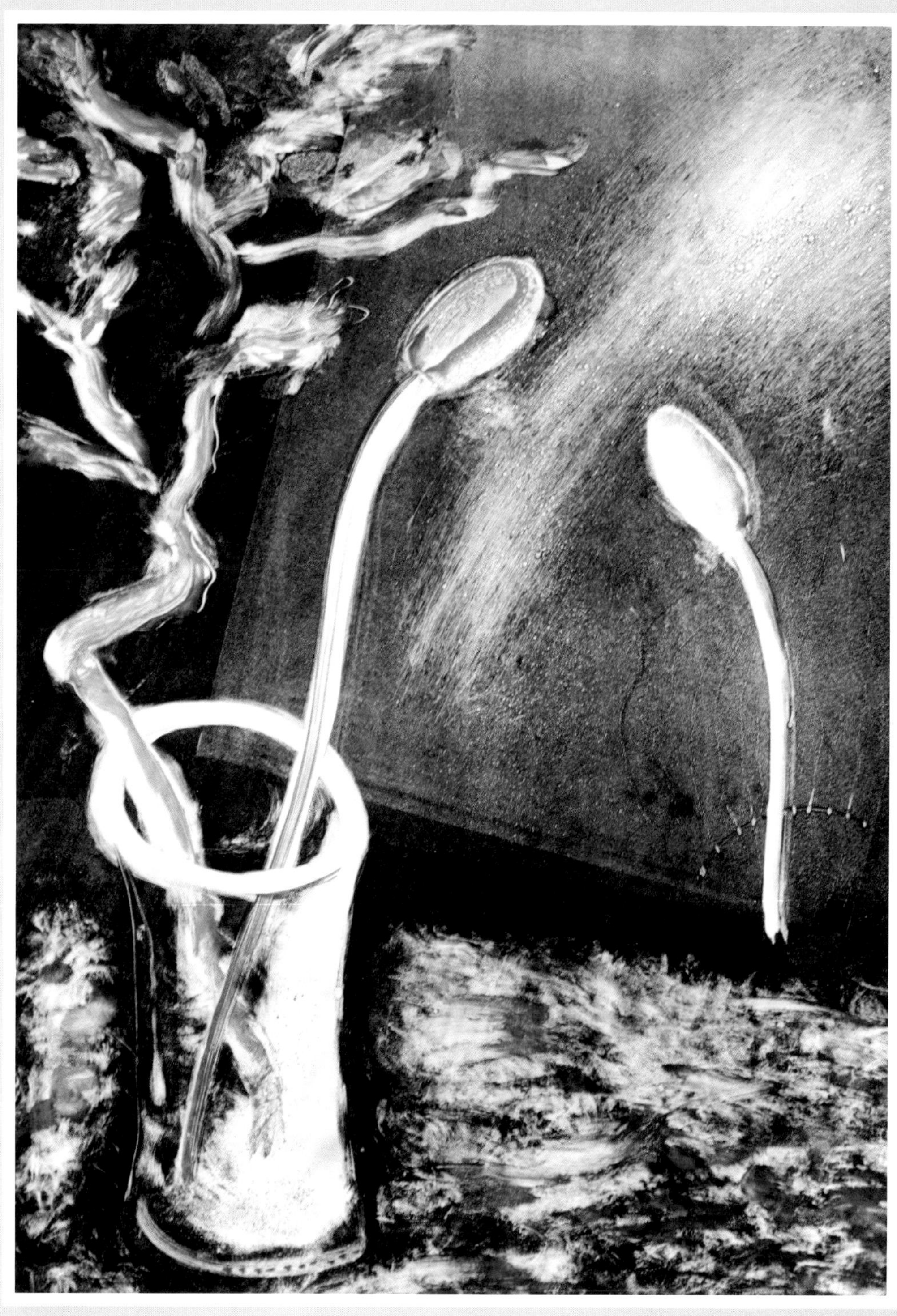

Flower and Mirror #1
1985
monoprint on paper
30 x 22 1/4 inches

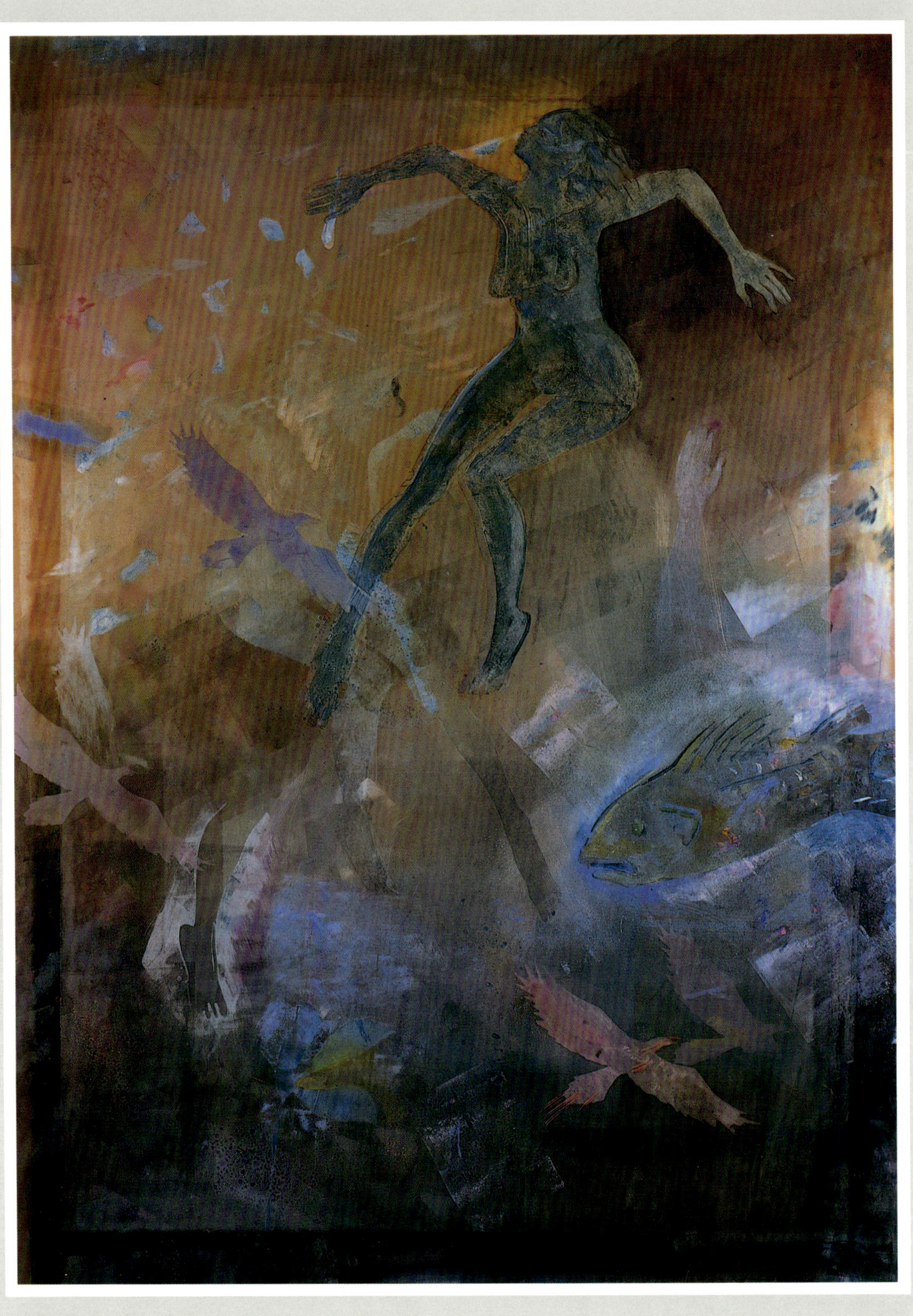

Figures Floating I
1985/86
oil on metal plate
47 x 36 inches

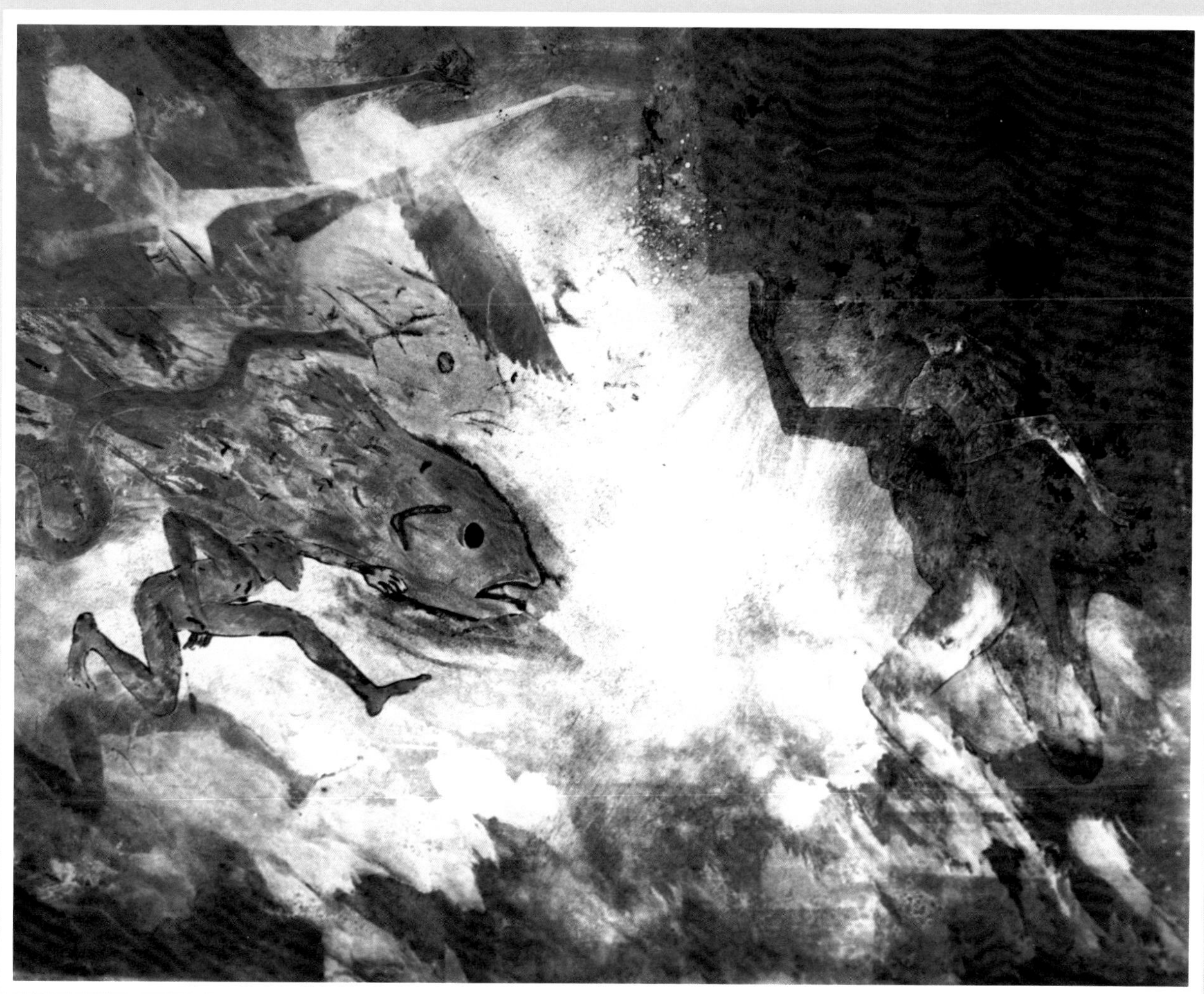

Leaper with Snake
1985
monoprint on paper
27 7/8 x 36 inches

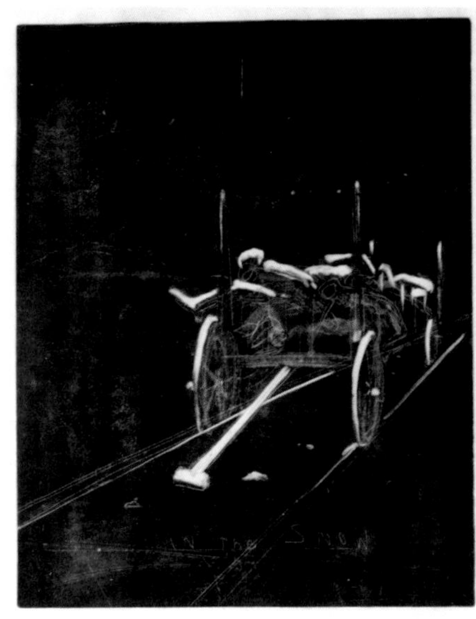
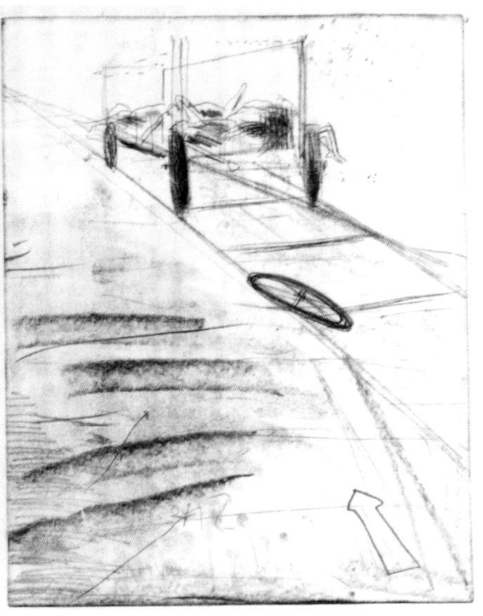
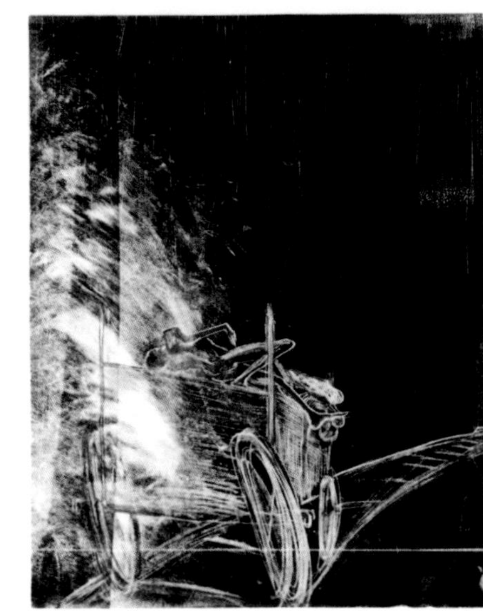
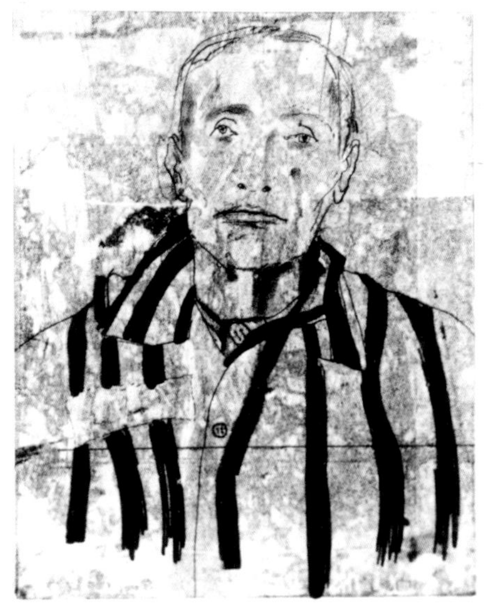

The Cart I
1986
monoprint on rice paper
25 1/2 x 38 1/2 inches

The Cart II
1986
monoprint on rice paper
24 1/4 x 39 1/2 inches

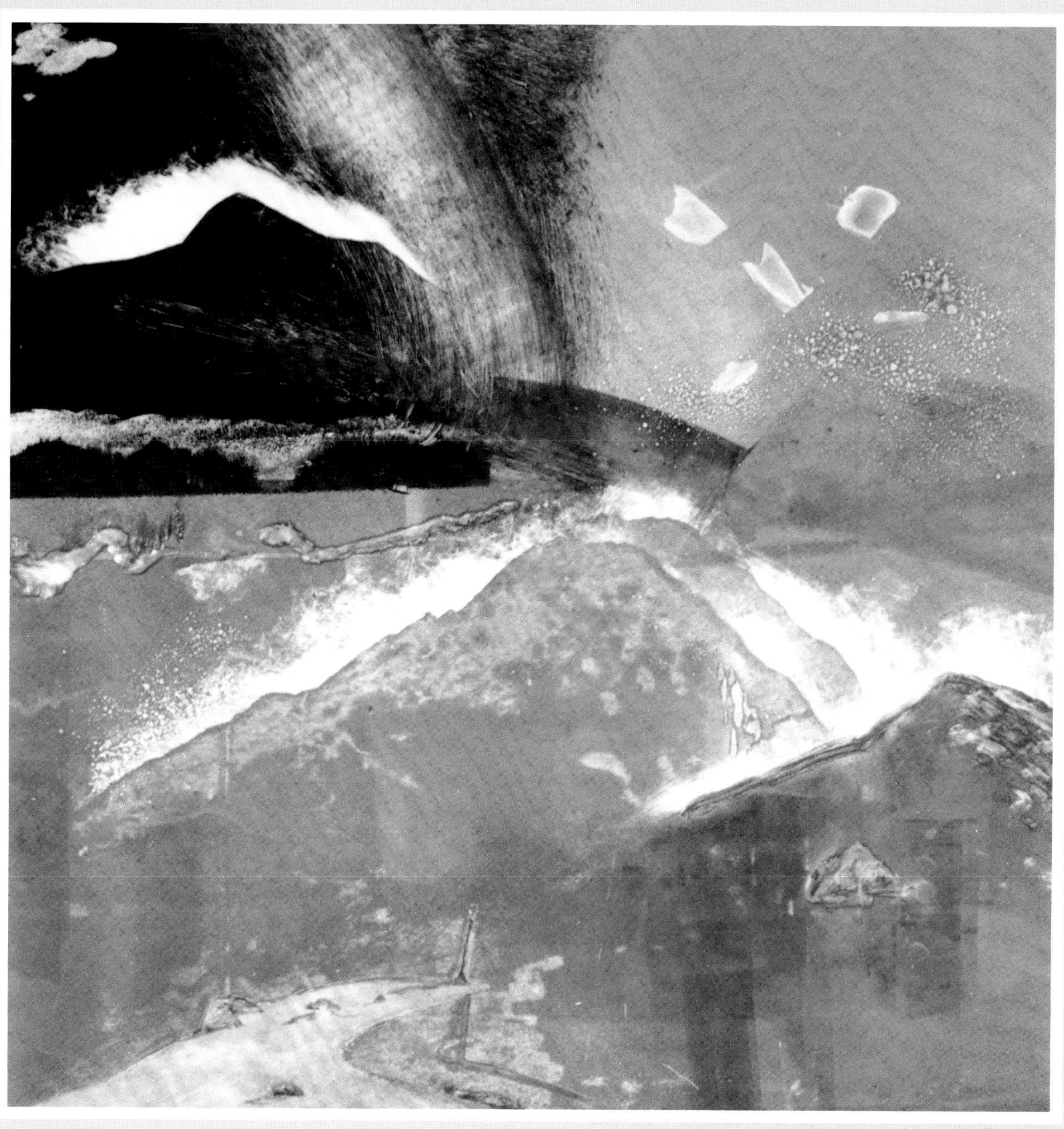

Site
1986
monoprint on paper
27 3/4 x 29 inches

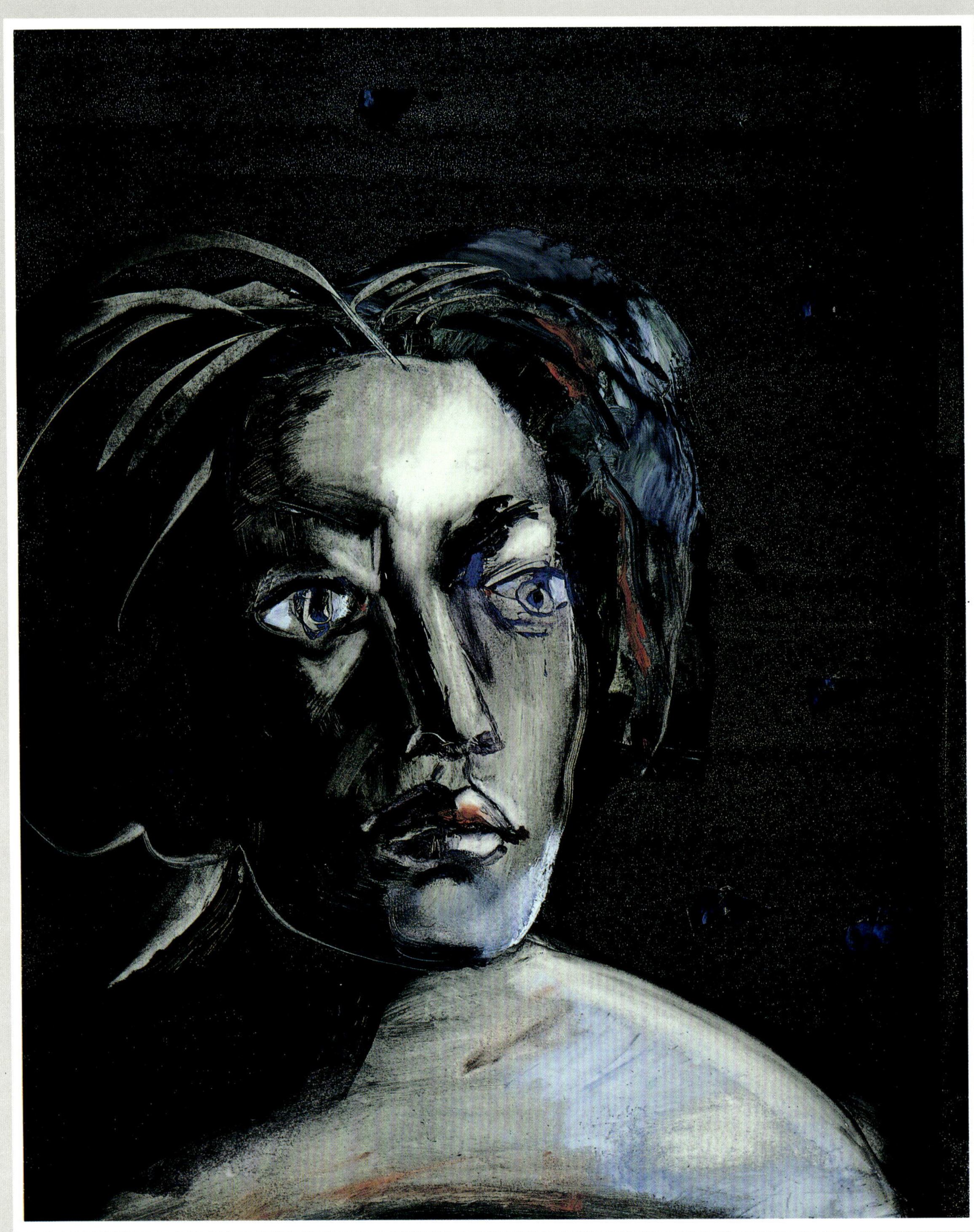

Mayan Head
1982
oil on paper
17 1/2 x 14 3/4 inches

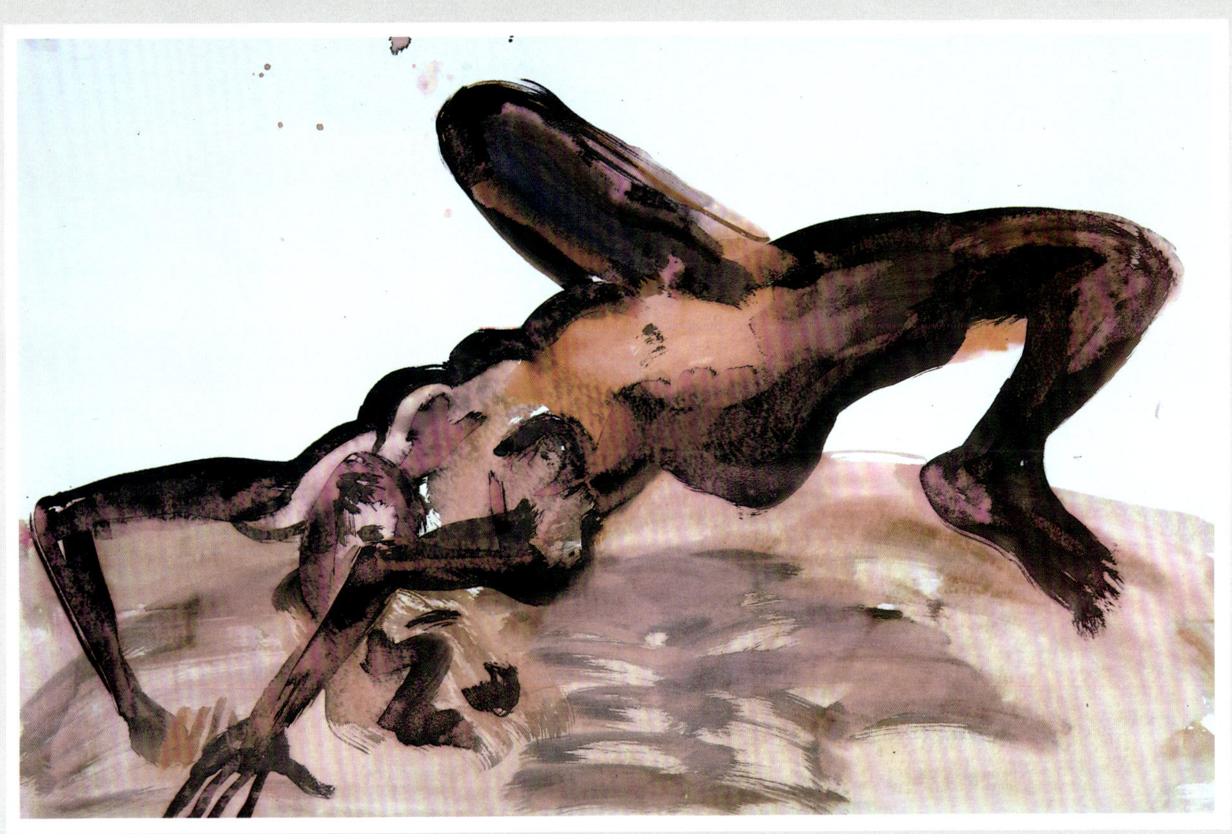

Reclining Woman
1985
ink on paper
26 1/8 x 40 inches

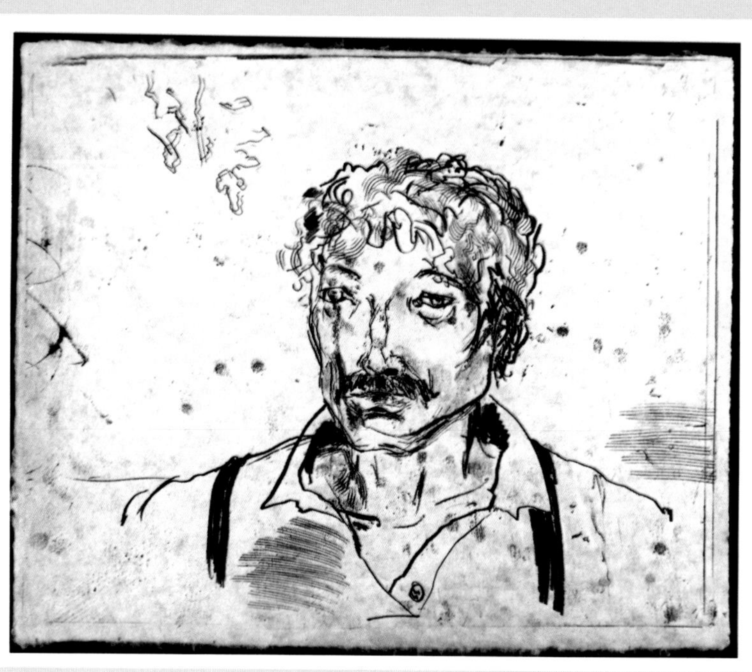

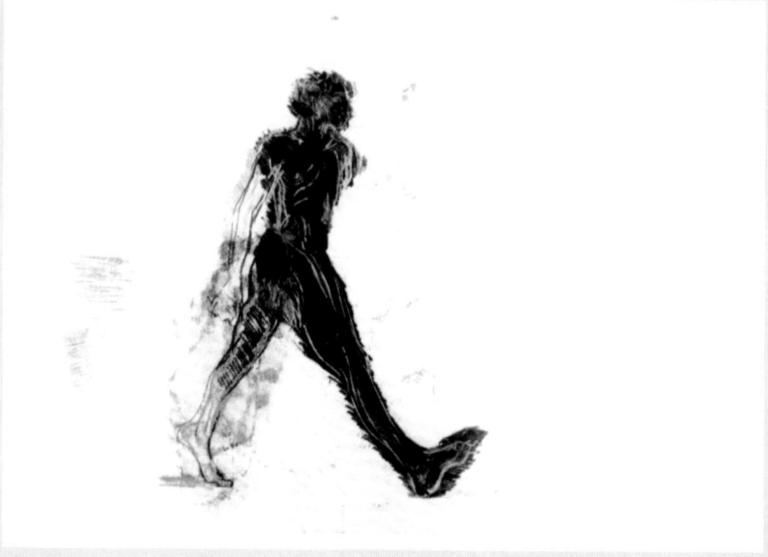

Leo
1987
monoprint on rice paper
17 x 20 5/8 inches

Man Walking with Orange Leg
1987
monoprint on rice paper
21 5/8 x 31 inches

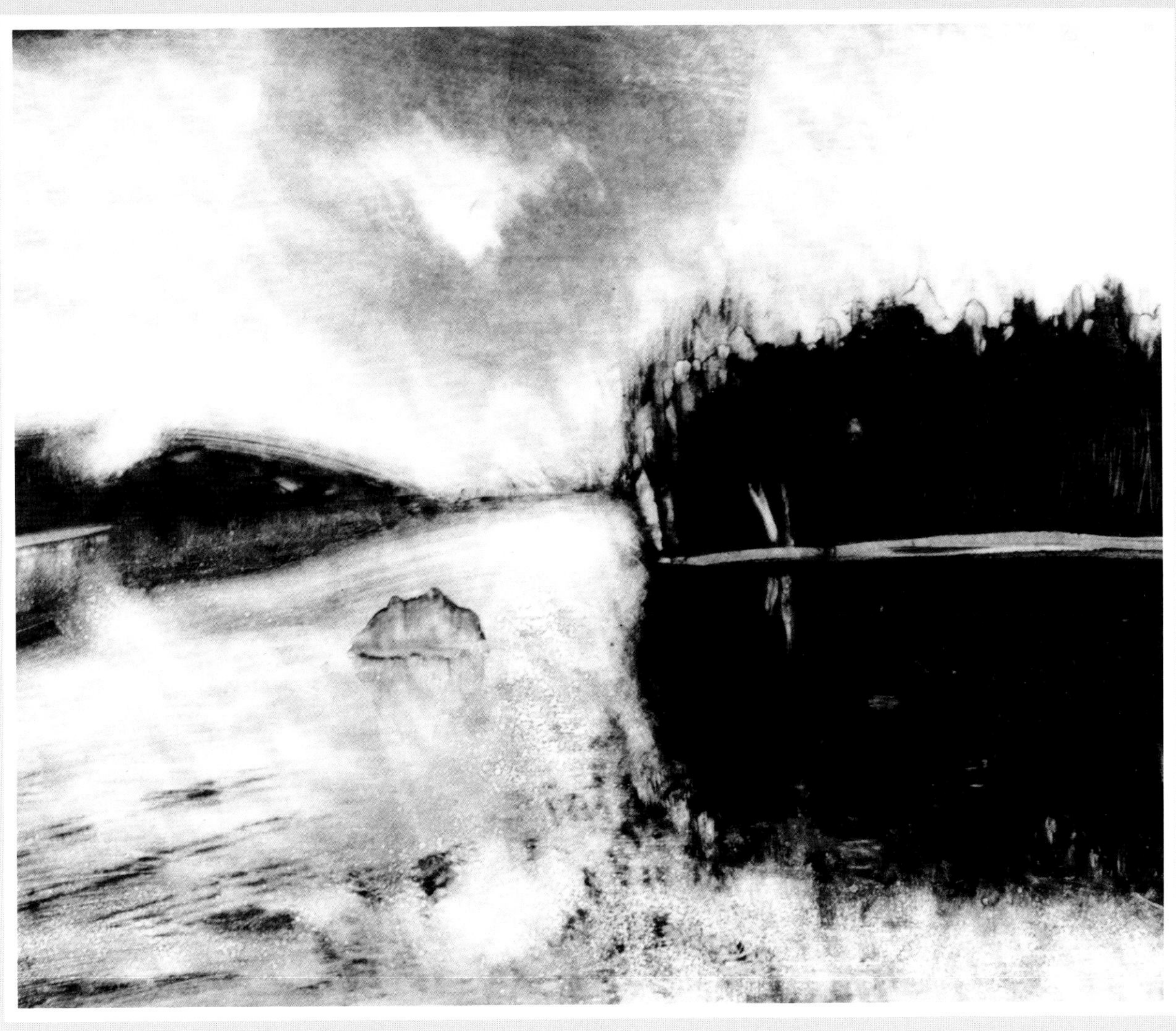

Cooper Lake IV
1987
monoprint on rice paper
17 x 21 inches

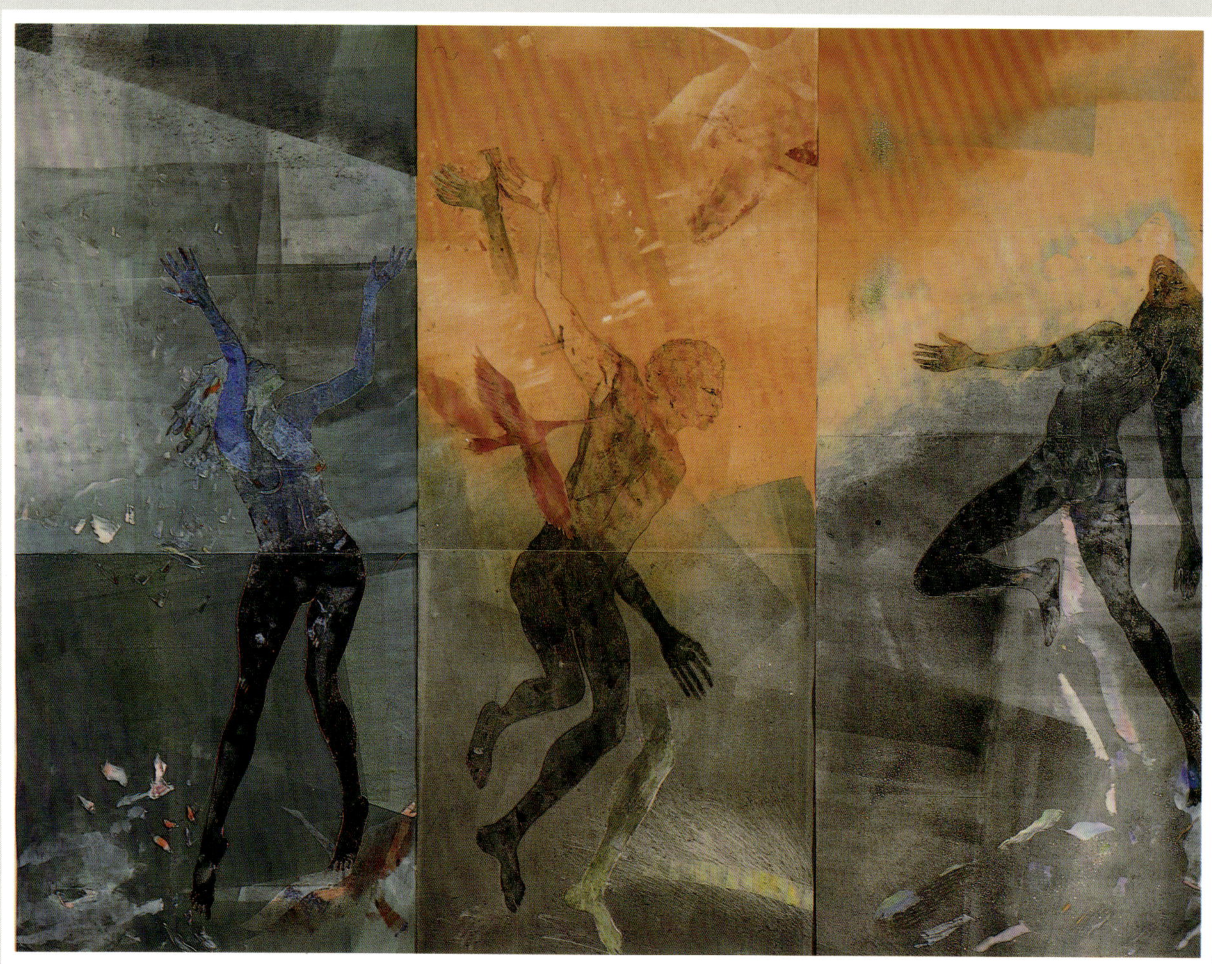

Left Half

The Time is Now
1985/86
monoprint (6 parts) on paper
63 x 165 inches

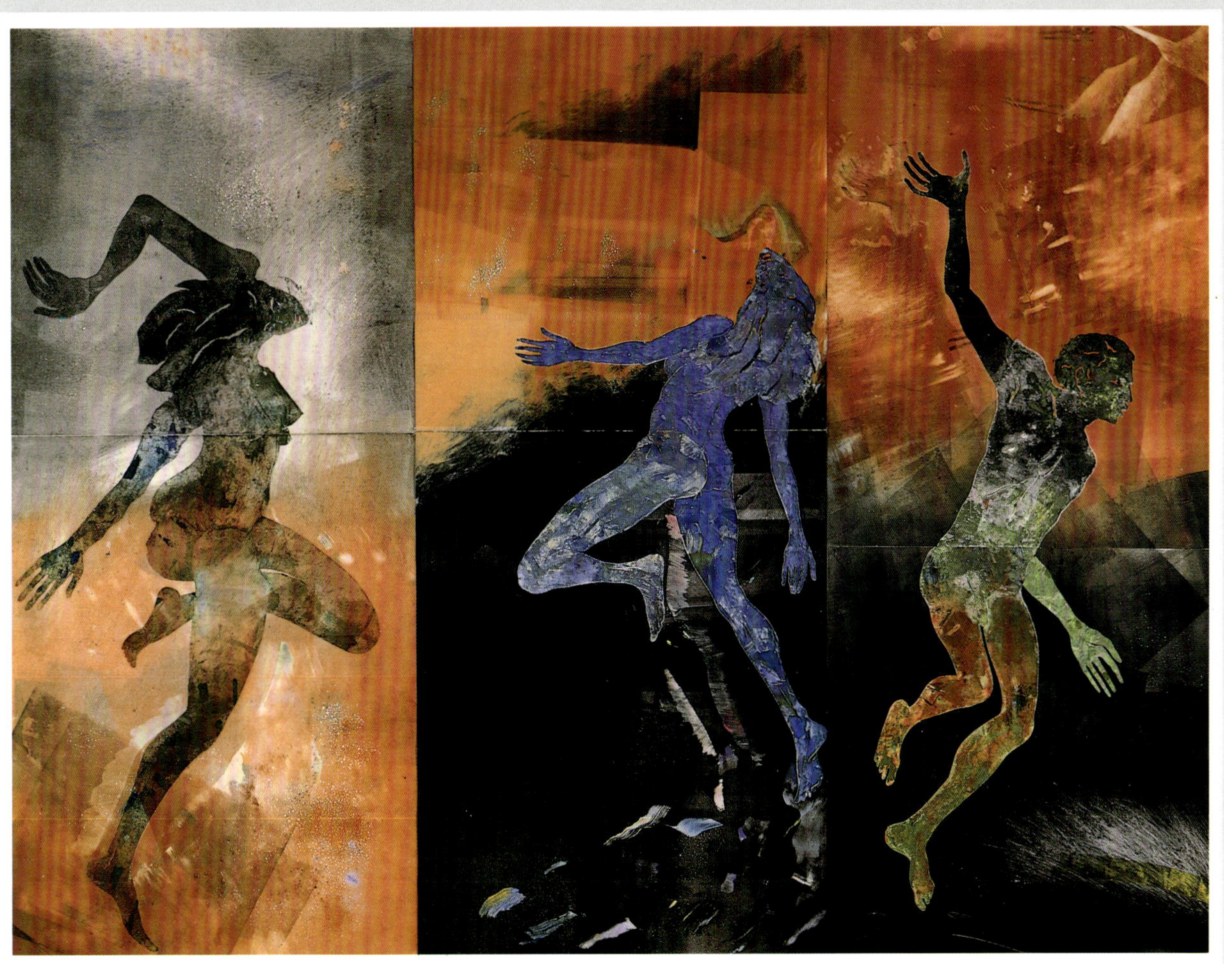

Right Half

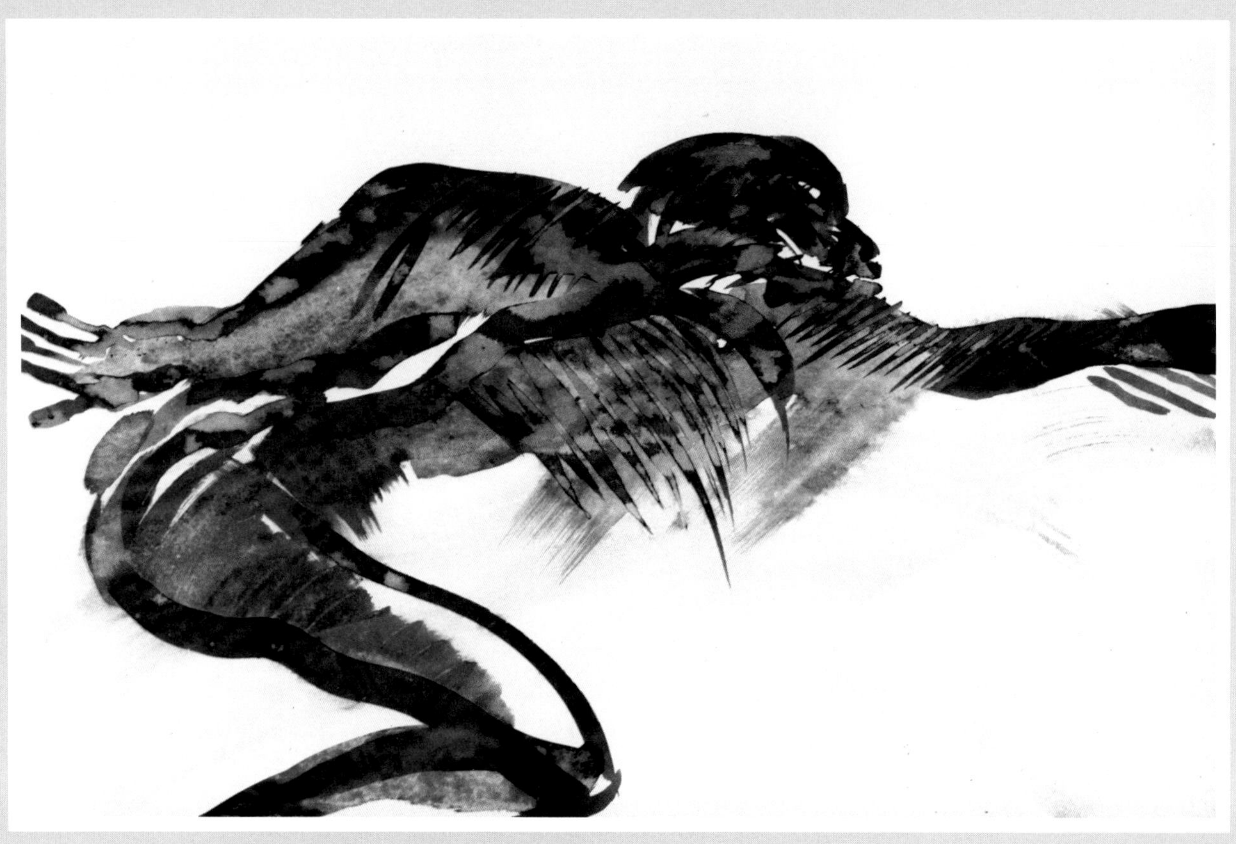

Swimmer
1979
ink on paper
23 1/8 x 35 inches

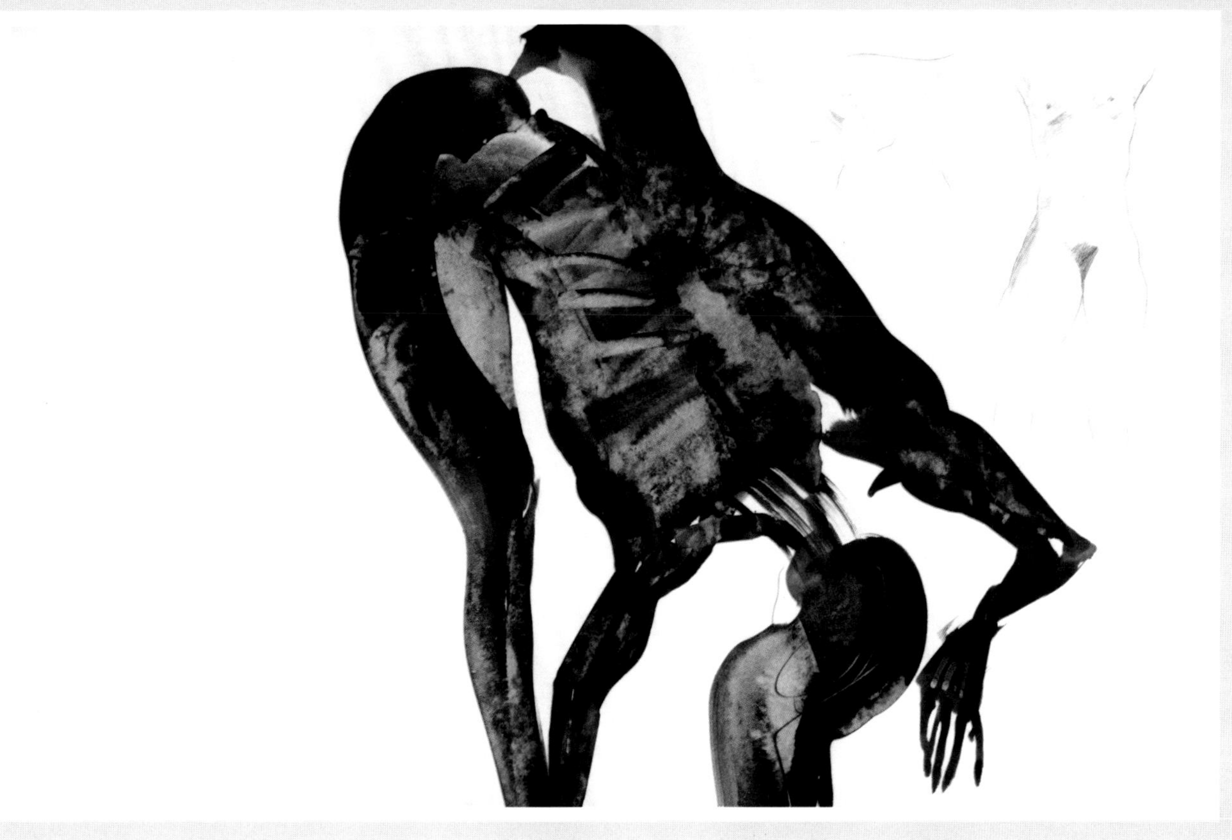

Woman: Leaning
1980
ink and pencil on paper
23 1/8 x 35 1/8 inches

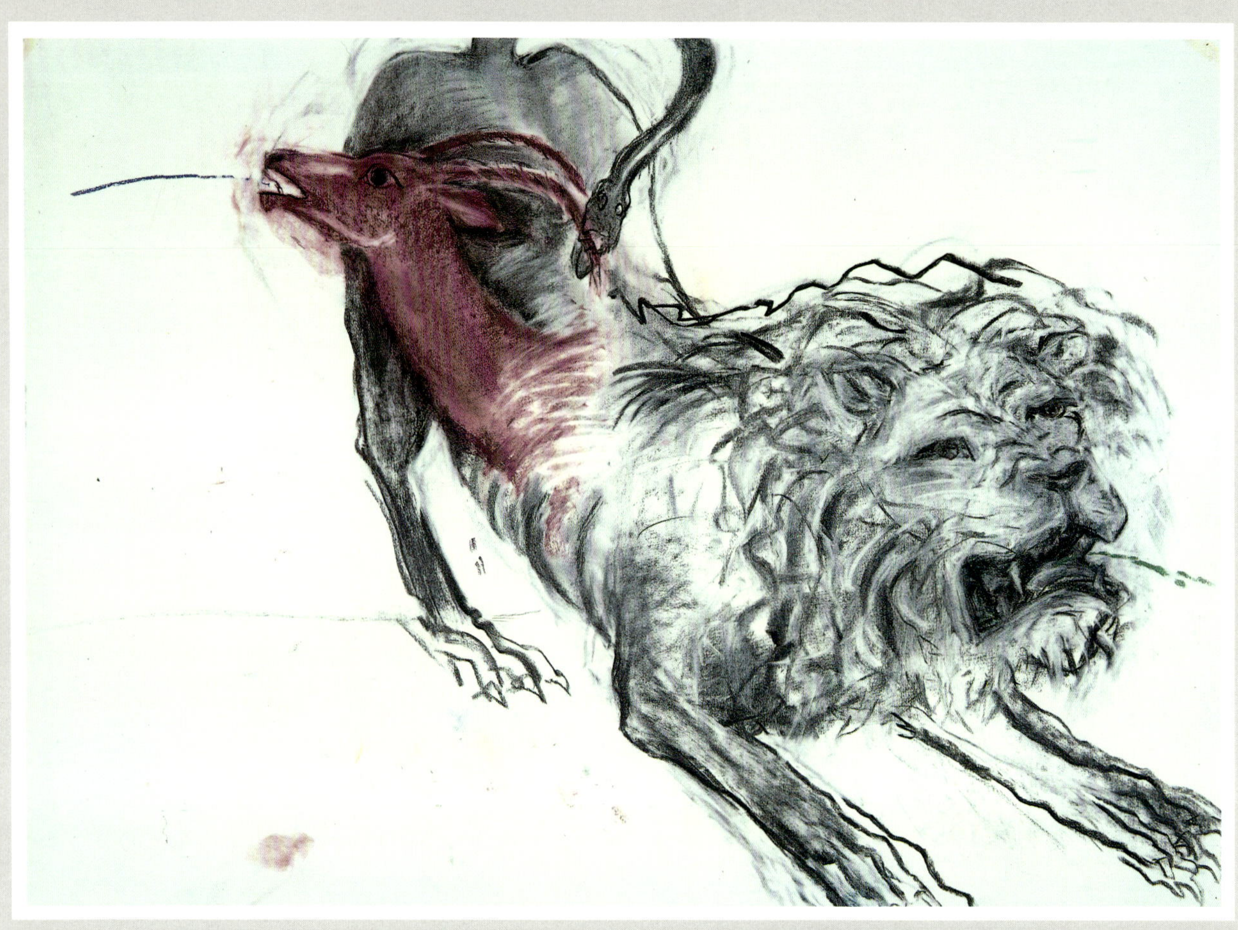

Chimera
1986
charcoal and pastel on paper
29 3/4 x 43 inches

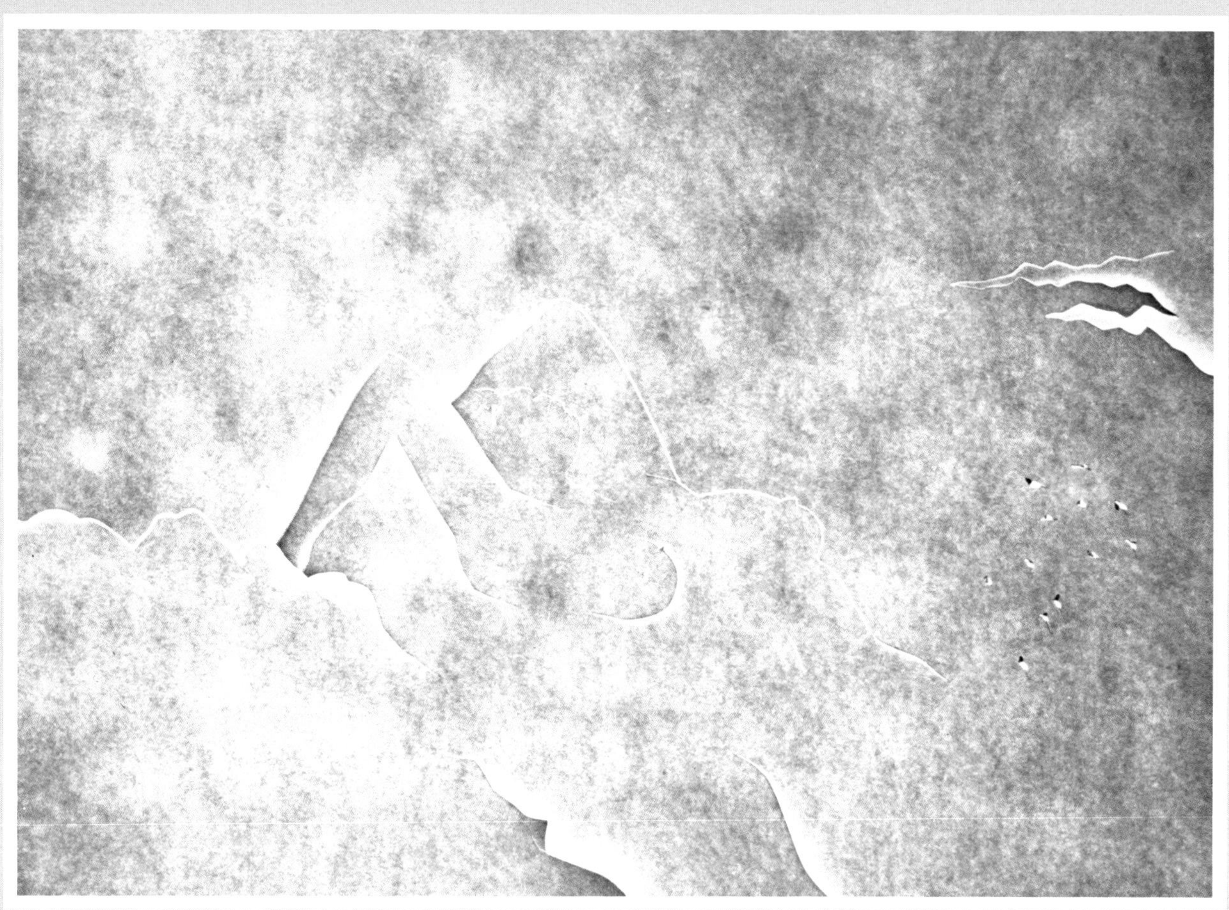

Untitled Shadow Paper
1980's
paper
12 x 17 inches

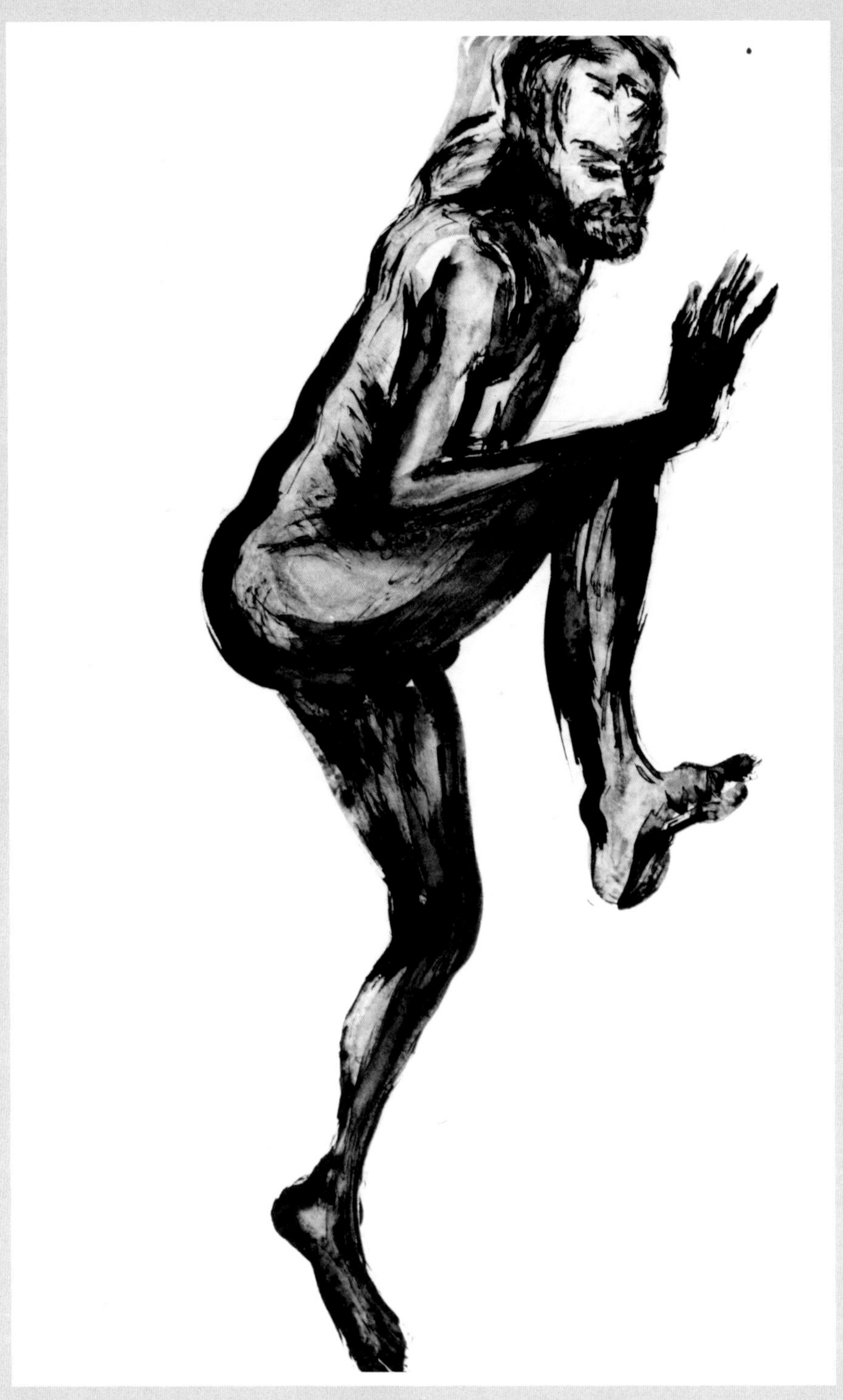

Man Jumping
1985
ink on paper
40 1/8 x 26 1/8 inches

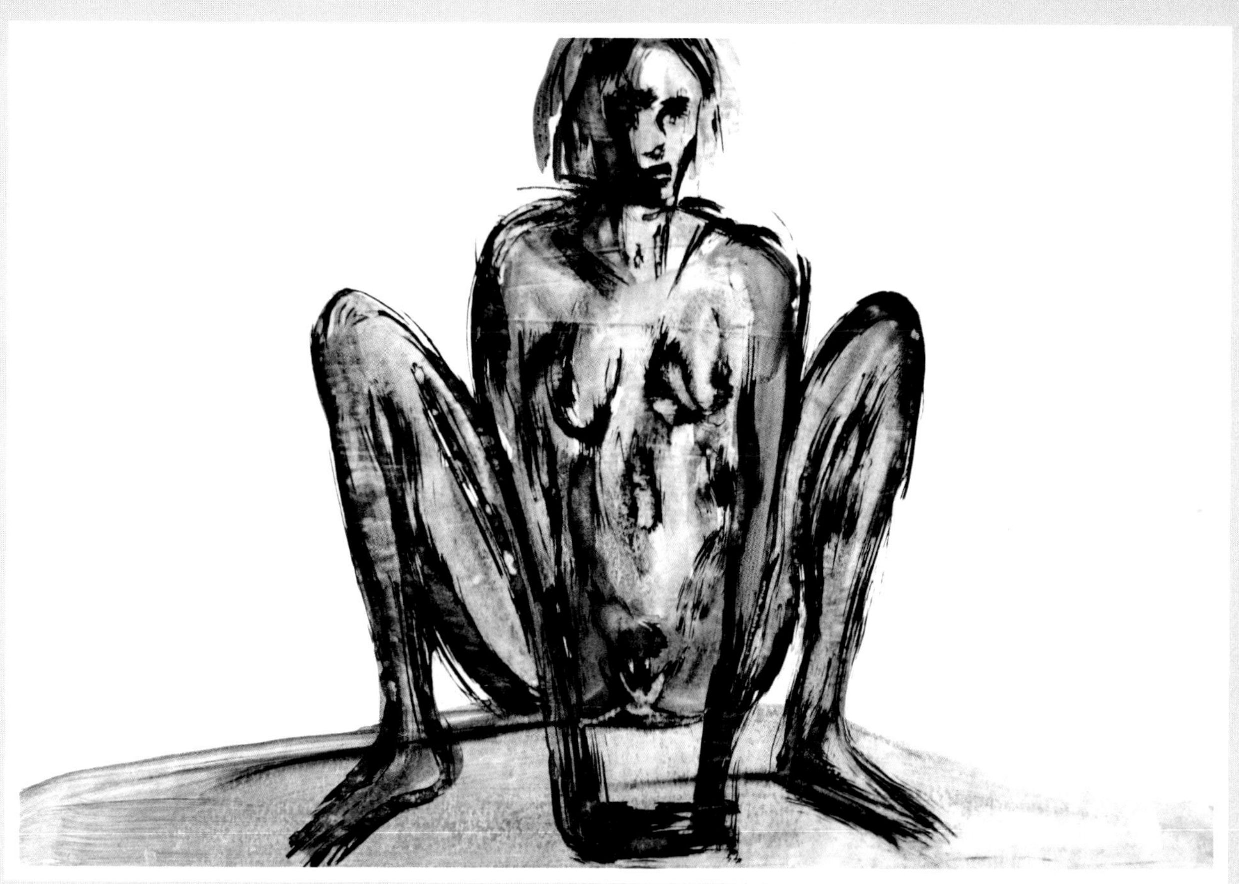

Crouching Woman
1984
ink on paper
25 3/4 x 37 7/8 inches

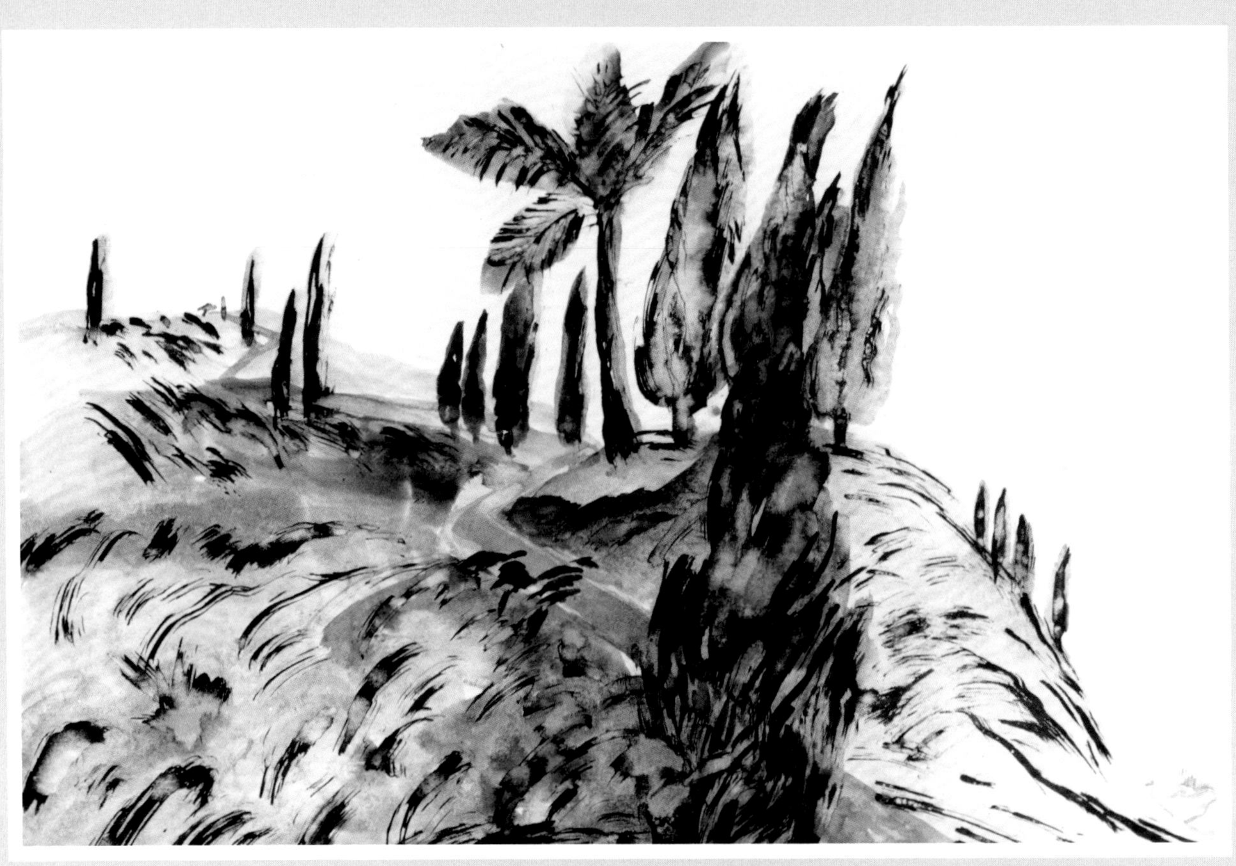

Jerusalem
1985
ink on paper
25 5/8 x 38 inches

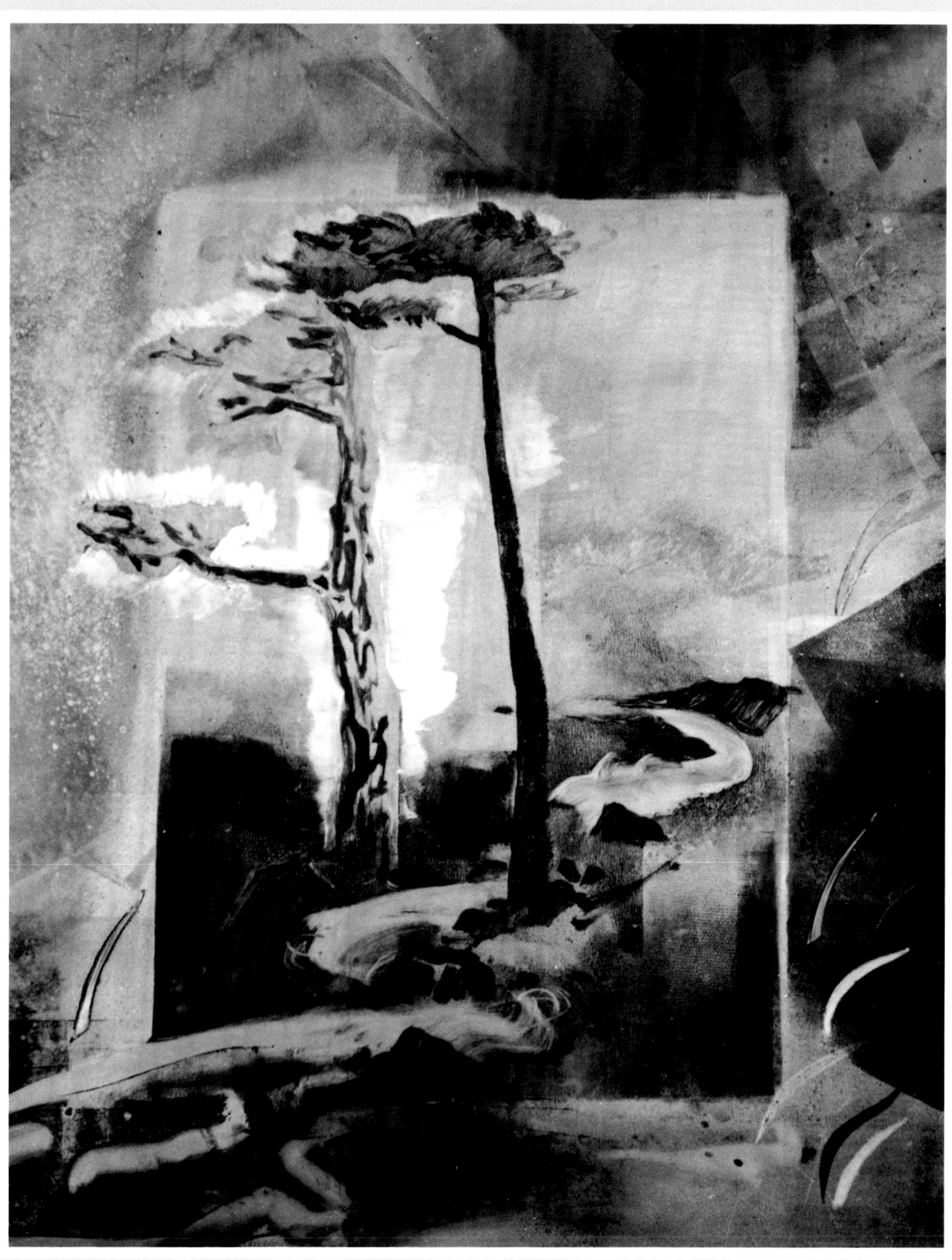

Landscape with Trees
1987
oil on metal plate
20 x 16 inches

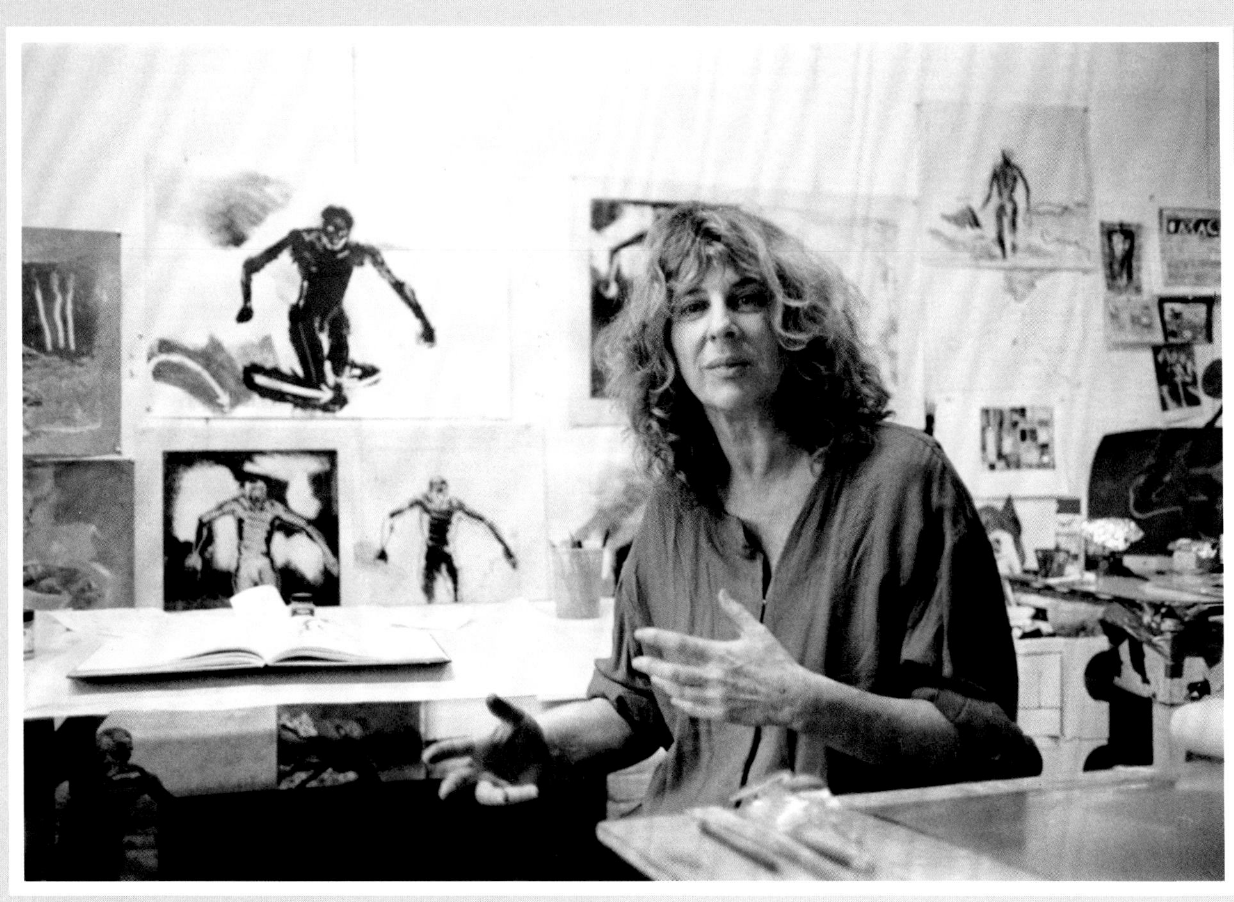

Mary Frank
in her studio,
December 1987

Chronology

1933	Born London to Eleanore Lockspeiser, a painter and Edward Lockspeiser, a musicologist and critic.
1940	Moves to United States with mother. Lives with maternal grandparents in Brooklyn for five years. Attends various public and private schools, including Friends School, The High School of Music and Art, and The Professional Children's School.
mid 1940's	Begins studying modern dance with Martha Graham. (Abandons dance training in 1950.)
1950	Graduates from The Professional Children's School. Marries Swiss photographer Robert Frank. Begins wood carving. Studies drawing with Max Beckmann at American Art School in New York City.
1951	Son Pablo born. Works intermittently at wood carving and plaster. Studies life drawing with Hans Hofmann. Begins lifetime commitment to drawing. Travels to Europe (France, Spain, Switzerland, England and Wales) with husband.
1952	Returns to New York City.
1953	Begins to visit Provincetown, Cape Cod in summers.
1954	Daughter Andrea Born. Returns to Hans Hofmann's drawing class. Meets Jan Muller, Robert Beauchamp, Miles Forst, Lester Johnson. Continues carving wood pieces and working in plaster.
1961	Ingram Merril Foundation Grant.
1962	Longview Foundation Grant.
1965-70	Teaches drawing at New School for Social Research.
1967	Gives up carving in wood. Concentrates on modelling in plaster. Begins making monoprints. Travels to Mexico.
1968	First of series of exhibitions at Zabriskie Gallery. Exhibits plaster and bronze sculpture. Illustrates first of three books. (*Enchanted*, by Elizabeth Coatsworth, Pantheon, 1968; *Buddha*, by Jean Cohen, Delacorte, 1969; *Son of-a-Mile-Long Mother*, by Alonzo Gibbs, Bobbs Merrill, 1970.) National Council of the Arts Award.
1969	Separates from Robert Frank (later divorces). Soon after, moves to Westbeth. Begins to concentrate on ceramic sculpture.
1970-75	Teaches sculpture and drawing at Queens College Graduate School.
1972	Buys summer house in Lakehill, NY. Travels to Mexico. American Academy and Institute of Arts and Letters Award in Art.
1973	New York State Creative Artists Public Service Grant. Guggenheim Fellowship for Graphics.
1975	Daughter Andrea dies.
1976	Visiting Artist, Skowhegan School of Painting and Sculpture.
1977	Travels to Paris for exhibition of her monoprints at Zabriskie's Paris Gallery. Brandeis University Creative Arts Award. Visits Morocco.

1978	Has major exhibition at the Neuberger Museum, State University of New York, College at Purchase, NY.
1981	Attends weekend workshops at Bread and Puppet Theater, Glover, VT.
1983	Guggenheim Award.
1984	Elected to the American Academy and Institute of Arts and Letters.
1985	Designs sets for the production *Big Mouth*, by Talking Band, performed at La Mama, New York.
1986	Lectures in *Artists' Visions* program at the 92nd Street Y, New York City. Designs sets for Brecht/Weill's "Little Mahagonny," performed at the 92nd Street Y.
1987	Commencement Speaker at the School of the Museum of Fine Arts in Boston.
1988	Has major exhibition at the DeCordova Museum, Lincoln, MA, which travels nationally.

Selected One-Person Exhibitions

1958	Poindexter Gallery, New York, NY
1961,63,66	Stephen Radich Gallery, New York, NY
1964	Drawing Shop Gallery, New York, NY
1965,67	Boris Mirski Gallery, Boston, MA
1968	*Mary Frank*, Zabriskie Gallery, New York, NY
1968	Donald Morris Gallery, Detroit, MI
1969	*Mary Frank/Drawing*, Richard Gray Gallery, Chicago, IL
1970	*Mary Frank*, Zabriskie Gallery, New York, NY
1971	*Mary Frank: Drawings*, Zabriskie Gallery, New York, NY
1973	*Mary Frank: Sculpture and Monoprints*, Zabriskie Gallery, New York, NY
1974	Bard College, Procter Art Center, Annandale-on-Hudson, NY
1975	*Mary Frank: Large Ceramic Sculpture*, Zabriskie Gallery, New York, NY
1975	*Mary Frank: Sculpture, Drawings, Prints*, Jorgensen Auditorium Gallery, University of Connecticut, Storrs, CT*
1976	*Mary Frank: Sculpture and Drawing*, Manwaring Gallery, Connecticut College, Cummings Art Center, New London, CT
1976	*Mary Frank: Recent Sculpture*, Harcus Krakow Rosen Sonnabend Gallery, Boston, MA
1976	*Mary Frank: Sculpture, Drawings, and Monoprints*, The Arts Club of Chicago, Chicago, IL
1976	Hobart College, Geneva, NY
1976	*Mary Frank: Drawings and Ceramic Sculpture*, Alice Simsar Gallery, Ann Arbor, MI

** A catalogue or brochure accompanied this exhibition.*

1976	*Exhibition of Sculpture and Drawings*, University of Bridgeport, Bridgeport, CT
1977	*Mary Frank*, Zabriskie Gallery, Paris, France and New York, NY
1978	*Mary Frank: Shadow Papers*, Zabriskie Gallery, New York, NY
1978	*Mary Frank: Sculpture/Drawings/Prints*, Neuberger Museum, Purchase, NY*
1978	*Mary Frank: Works on Paper*, Neuberger Museum, Purchase, NY (traveling exhibition)*
1979	*Mary Frank: Sculpture and Monoprints*, Zabriskie Gallery, New York, NY*
1981	*Mary Frank: 1980-81*, Zabriskie Gallery, New York, NY*
1981/82	*Mary Frank: Sculpture and Monotypes*, Zabriskie Gallery, New York, NY*
1982	Makler Gallery, Philadelphia, PA
1984	*Mary Frank: Monotypes and Sculpture*, Zabriskie Gallery, New York, NY*
1984	*Mary Frank: Sculpture and Monotypes*, Quay Gallery, San Francisco, CA
1985	*Mary Frank: Monoprints*, Marsha Mateyka Gallery, Washington, D.C.
1986	*Mary Frank: Sculpture and Works on Paper*, Zabriskie Gallery, New York, NY*
1987	Mary Frank: Persephone Studies, The Brooklyn Museum, Brooklyn, NY*
1987	*Mary Frank: Drawings and Monoprints*, Roger Ramsay Gallery, Chicago, IL
1988	*Natural Histories: Mary Frank's Sculpture, Prints, and Drawings*, DeCordova Museum, Lincoln, MA (traveling to Everson Museum of Art and Pennsylvania Academy of The Fine Arts)*
1988	*Mary Frank: Works on Paper 1970-1987*, Nielsen Gallery, Boston, MA

Selected Group Exhibitons

1972	*10 Independents*, The Solomon R. Guggenheim Museum, New York, NY*
1972	*American Woman Artists' Show*, Gedok, Hamburg, W. Germany
1972	Whitney Sculpture Annual, Whitney Museum of American Art, New York, NY*
1973	*1973 Biennial Exhibition: Contemporary American Art,* Whitney Biennial, Whitney Museum of American Art, New York, NY*
1974	*Focus on Woman*, Philadelphia, PA
1975	*Masterworks in Wood*, Portland Art Museum, Portland, OR*
1975	*Three Centuries of the American Nude*, New York Cultural Center, New York, NY; Minneapolis Institute of Arts, Minneapolis, MN; University of Houston Fine Arts Center, Houston, TX*
1976	*American Artists '76: A Celebration*, Marion Koogler McNay Art Institute, San Antonio, TX*

** A catalogue or brochure accompanied this exhibition.*

1976	*Private Notations: Artists' Sketchbooks*, Philadelphia College of Art, Philadelphia, PA*
1977	*Drawings of the 70's* The Art Institute of Chicago, Chicago, IL*
1978	*Figure in the Landscape*, Wave Hill, Riverdale, NY
1978	*Perspective '78: Works by Women*, Albright College, Reading, PA*
1978	*8 Artists*, Philadelphia Museum of Art, Philadelphia, PA*
1979	Whitney Biennial, Whitney Museum of American Art, New York, NY*
1979	*By the Sea: 20th Century Americans at the Shore*, The Queens Museum, Flushing, NY*
1980	*The Narrative Impulse,* Hayden Gallery, Massachusetts Institute of Technology, Cambridge, MA*
1980	*The Figurative Tradition*, Whitney Museum of American Art, New York, NY*
1980	*The Painterly Print*, Metropolitan Museum of Art, New York, NY*
1980	*Sculpture in the 70's—The Figure*, Pratt Institute, New York, NY*
1980	*On Paper*, Institute of Contemporary Art, Virginia Museum, Richmond,VA*
1980	*Mysterious and Magical Realism*, The Aldrich Museum of Contemporary Art, Ridgefield, CT*
1981	*Tracking the Marvelous*, Grey Art Gallery, New York University, New York, NY*
1981	*The Human Form: Interpretations*, The Maryland Institute, College of Art, Baltimore, MD
1981	*The Clay Figure*, American Craft Museum, New York, NY
1983	*Bronze Sculpture in the Landscape*, Wave Hill, Riverdale, NY*
1983	*Fragmentations*, The New Britain Museum of American Art, New Britain, CT*
1983	*American Printmaker's Show*, The Brooklyn Museum, Brooklyn, NY*
1985	*Contemporary Monotypes: Six Masters*, De Saisset Museum, Santa Clara, CA*
1985	*Contemporary American Monotypes*, The Chrysler Museum, Norfolk, VA*
1985	*Body and Soul: Recent Figurative Sculpture*, Contemporary Arts Center, Cincinnati, OH*
1985	*Clay*, Dayton Art Institute, Dayton, OH*
1986	*Disarming Images*, Contemporary Arts Center, Cincinnati, OH (traveled nationally through 1986)*
1986	*Figure as Subject: The Last Decade*, Whitney Museum at Equitable Center, New York, NY*
1986	*Tenth Anniversary Exhibition*, Marilyn Pearl Gallery, New York, NY
1986	*Public and Private: American Prints Today*, The Brooklyn Museum, Brooklyn, NY*
1987	*Sculpture of the Eighties*, The Queens Museum, Flushing, NY*
1987	Anne Weber Gallery, Georgetown, ME

** A catalogue or brochure accompanied this exhibition.*

1987	*Recent Figurative Prints*, Associated American Artists, New York, NY*
1987	*The Eloquent Object*, Philbrook Art Center, Tulsa, OK (traveling nationally 1988-89)*
1987	*American Ceramics Now*, Everson Museum, Syracuse, NY (traveling nationally)*
1987	*Standing Ground: Sculpture by American Women,* The Contemporary Arts Center, Cincinnati, OH*
1987	*Pastel Anthology II*, Grace Borgenicht Gallery, New York, NY

Selected Public Collections

The Museum of Modern Art, New York, NY
The Metropolitan Museum of Art, New York, NY
Whitney Museum of American Art, New York, NY
Des Moines Art Center, Des Moines, IA
Neuberger Museum, Purchase, NY
The Art Institute of Chicago, Chicago, IL
Kalamazoo Institute of Arts, Kalamazoo, MI
University of Massachusetts
University of New Mexico
Worcester Art Museum, Worcester, MA
Yale University Art Gallery, New Haven, CT
Southern Illinois University
Hirshhorn Museum and Sculpture Garden, Washington, D.C.
Brown University, Providence, RI
Akron Art Museum, Akron, OH
Michael C. Rockefeller Arts Center Gallery, Fredonia, NY
Arnot Art Museum, Elmira, NY
Storm King Art Center, Mountainville, NY
Crocker Bank, Chicago, IL
Bank of Chicago, Chicago, IL
Everson Museum of Art of Syracuse and Onondaga County, Syracuse, NY
Library of Congress, Washington, D.C.
Virginia Museum of Fine Arts, Richmond, VA
University of North Carolina, Chapel Hill, NC
Museum of Fine Arts, Boston, MA
The Pennsylvania Academy of the Fine Arts, Philadelphia, PA
The Brooklyn Museum, Brooklyn, NY
Museo Rufino Tamayo, Mexico City,Mexico

Selected Bibliography

Valerie Peterson, "Mary Frank: Sculptures a Bridge for Ideas," *Art News*, January, 1963, 34-5.

Hilton Kramer, "The Possibilities of Mary Frank," *Arts*, March, 1963, 50-5.

James R. Mellow, "Keeping the Figure Vital," *The New York Times*, September 15, 1968, D 33.

Hilton Kramer, "The Sculpture of Mary Frank: Poetical, Metaphorical, Interior," *The New York Times*, February 22, 1970, II, 27

Gerrit Henry, "The Clay Landscapes of Mary Frank," *Crafts Horizon*, December, 1971, 18-21.

James R. Mellow, "About Woman as a Sexual Being," *The New York Times*, April 22, 1973, II, 19.

April Kingsley, "Mary Frank: A Sense of Timelessness," *Art News*, Summer, 1973, 65-7.

James R. Mellow, "Mary Frank Explores Women's Erotic Fantasies," *The New York Times*, January 19, 1975, II, 23.

Hilton Kramer, "Art: Sensual Serene Sculpture," *The New York Times*, January 25, 1975, 23.

Hilton Kramer, *The Sculpture of Mary Frank*, published by the Eakins Press Foundation, 1975.

Jane Holtz Kay, "Mythic Fragments," *Art News*, Summer, 1976, 137.

Martica Sawin, "The Sculpture of Mary Frank," *Arts*, March, 1977, 130-132.

Hayden Herrera, "Myth and Metamorphosis: The Work of Mary Frank," *Arts Canada*, April - May, 1978, 15-26.

Vivien Raynor, "Sculptural Marvels of Mary Frank," *The New York Times*, June 16, 1978, III, 1.

Robert Hughes, "Images of Metamorphosis," *Time*, July 10, 1978, 76.

Carter Ratcliff, "Mary Frank's Monotypes," *The Print Collector's Newsletter*, November - December, 1978, 151-154.

Eleanor Munro, "Mary Frank," *Originals: American Women Artists*, Simon and Schuster, 1979, 289-308.

Garth Clark, *A Century of Ceramics*, Dutton, 1979.

Jon R. Friedman, "Mary Frank," *Arts Magazine*, September, 1979, 12.

Helen A. Harrison, "A Sensual and Enigmatic World," *The New York Times*, December 23, 1979, XXI, 15.

Hilton Kramer, "Art: World of the Monotype Inaugurates a Corner at Met," *The New York Times*, October 24, 1980, III, 1.

Calvin Goodman, "Monotype - a Singular Art Form," *American Artist*, January, 1981, 58-63.

Grace Glueck, "The Clay Figure at the Craft Museum," *The New York Times*, February 20, 1981, III, 21.

Paul Cummings, "Interview: Mary Frank Talks with Paul Cummings," *Drawing Magazine*, May/June, 1981, 11-14.

Elizabeth Hess, "Female Parts," *Village Voice*, May 6-12, 1981.

Hilton Kramer, "Mary Frank," *The New York Times*, May 15, 1981, III, 21.

Reagan Upshaw, "Mary Frank at Zabriskie," *Art in America*, October, 1981, 140.

Hayden Herrera, "Mary Frank," Zabriskie Gallery Catalogue, 1983.

Gerrit Henry, "Mary Frank," *Art News*, May, 1983, 160.

Ilene Susan Fort, "Mary Frank," *Arts*, May, 1983, 62.

Michael Brenson, "Mary Frank," *The New York Times*, November 30, 1984, III, 23.

Estella Lauter, *Women as Mythmakers: Poetry and Visual Art by Twentieth-Century Women*, Indiana University Press, Bloomington, 1984, pp 144-146.

William Zimmer, Review of 10th Anniversary Exhibition at Marilyn Pearl Gallery, *The New York Times*, October 24, 1986, III, 28.

John McDonald Moore, "The Drawings of Mary Frank," *Drawing*, January - February, 1986, 97-101.

Lawrence Campbell, "Mary Frank," *Art in America*, March, 1987, 139-40.

Vivien Raynor, "Persephone Studies at the Brooklyn Museum," *The New York Times*, March 27, 1987, III, 25.

Margaret Moorman, "In a Timeless World," *Art News*, May, 1987, 90-98.

Linda Konheim Kramer, "Mary Frank: Persephone Studies," *American Ceramics*, Fall, 1987, 17-21.

(exhibition catalogues are listed under selected exhibitions.)

Checklist

Unless otherwise noted, all works are lent courtesy of the artist and Zabriskie Gallery.

All dimensions are in inches. Height precedes width precedes depth.

Sculptures

In describing her clay sculpture, Mary Frank prefers the use of the generic term, ceramic.

1. **Standing Woman**, 1980
ceramic
37 x 12 x 15

2. **Woman Lying Down**, 1980
ceramic
11 3/4 x 39 x 84
Courtesy of The Pennsylvania Academy of the Fine Arts, Philadelphia, Gilpin Fund Purchase

3. **Walking Woman,** 1981
plaster and branches
65 x 61 x 57

4. **Running Man**, 1981
plaster and branches
63 1/2 x 25 1/2 x 45

5. **Pieta**, 1981
ceramic
36 3/4 x 28 1/2 x 17

6. **Three Dancers**, 1981
ceramic
25 1/2 x 34 x 25

7. **Crouching Woman with Two Faces**, 1981
ceramic
29 x 24 x 16
Collection of Mr. Richard Ekstract

8. **Horse and Rider**, 1982
ceramic
24 x 43 x 31 1/2
Collection Everson Museum of Art, Syracuse, NY; Museum Purchase, with funds from the J. Stanley Coyne Foundation

9. **Utterance**, 1984
ceramic
39 1/2 x 18 x 26
Collection of Mr. and Mrs. Carter P. Thacher

10. **Persephone**, 1985
ceramic
25 x 74 x 38
Courtesy Zabriskie Gallery

11. **Chimera**, 1984-86
papier mache
34 x 60 x 24

12. **Head**, 1985/86
bronze
28 x 34 x 22

13. **Ethiopian**, 1986/87
ceramic with oil paint
27 1/2 x 20 x 14

The following small sculptures date from between 1979-87.

14. **Bird**
ceramic
6 x 6 x 1/2

15. **Man and Wildebeest**
raku
4 1/2 x 5 x 2

16. **Natural History**
raku
3 1/4 x 5 1/2 x 1

17. **Imprint**
ceramic
5 1/4 x 10 3/4 x 1/4

18. **Hand and Dinosaur**
ceramic
3 1/2 x 5 1/2 x 3/4

19. **Seated Woman**
raku with glaze
6 3/4 x 3 3/4 x 3 1/4

20. **Seated Woman on Throne**
bronze
6 3/4 x 3 1/2 x 4

21. **Man with Mask**
bronze
3 3/4 x 5 3/4 x 3 3/4
Collection of Leo Treitler

22. **Woman with Baby**
bronze
5 3/4 x 4 x 2
Collection of Leo Treitler

23. **Famine**
ceramic
6 3/4 x 4 1/4 x 7 1/2
Collection of Leo Treitler

24. **Figure with Hand**
ceramic
6 x 2 1/4 x 2 1/2
Collection of Leo Treitler

25. **Woman in Garden**
ceramic
4 1/4 x 4 x 2 1/2

26. **Woman in Wind**
ceramic
6 x 1 1/2 x 2 1/4

27. **Figure and Wave**
ceramic
2 x 11 3/4 x 3 1/2

Plaster Reliefs

28. **Woman and Wave**, 1982
plaster, ceramic, glass and oil
42 1/2 x 32 1/2 x 2 1/4
Private Collection

29. **Horses**, 1982
plaster, ceramic, glass, and oil
23 x 31 x 4 3/4

30. **Passage**, 1986
plaster, oil paint
18 1/2 x 28

31. **The Cart**, 1986
plaster, oil paint
18 1/2 x 28

Monoprints

Although Mary Frank's prints have often been referred to as monotypes, which can be defined as unique, unrepeatable images that lack a fixed matrix, the artist prefers the use of the term monoprint.

1. **Poppies**, 1979
monoprint on paper
26 x 38

2. **The Storm is Here**, 1982
monoprint and drypoint on paper
23 3/4 x 35 3/8

3. **Spirit Riders**, 1982
monoprint on paper
29 1/2 x 40 5/8

4. **The Storm is Here**, 1982
monoprint and drypoint on paper
23 3/4 x 35 1/4

5. **Man with Wings**, 1982
monoprint on paper
page: 33 x 29 1/2

6. **Pandemonium**, 1983
monoprint on paper
27 5/8 x 27 3/4

7. **Chase**, 1983
monoprint (diptych) on paper
25 3/8 x 35 1/2 (left); 25 1/2 x 35 1/2 (right)

8. **Utterance,** 1983
monoprint on paper
33 x 25 1/2

9. **Lovers**, 1983
monoprint on paper
23 3/4 x 26 3/8

10. **Leap**, 1984
monoprint on paper
36 x 27 7/8
Collection of Leo Treitler

11. **Centaur**, 1984
monoprint on paper
27 7/8 x 35 7/8

12. **Recognition**, 1984
monoprint on paper
27 5/8 x 36 1/2

13. **Suspension**, 1984
monoprint on paper
27 7/8 x 35 7/8

14. **At the Edge**, 1984
monoprint on rice paper
25 1/4 x 38 3/4

15. **Leaper with Snake**, 1985
monoprint on paper
27 7/8 x 36

16. **Flower and Mirror #1**, 1985
monoprint on paper
30 x 22 1/4

17. **Poppies**, 1985
monoprint on paper
17 3/8 x 25 1/4

18. **The Time is Now**, 1985/86
monoprint (6 parts) on paper
63 x 165

19. **The Cart I**, 1986
monoprint on rice paper
25 1/2 x 38 1/2

20. **The Cart II**, 1986
monoprint on rice paper
24 1/4 x 39 1/2

21. **Site**, 1986
monoprint on paper
27 3/4 x 29

22. **Passages**, 1986
monoprint on rice paper
28 1/8 x 72

23. **Cooper Lake I**, 1987
monoprint on rice paper
17 x 20 3/4

24. **Cooper Lake II**, 1987
monoprint on rice paper
17 x 20 5/8

25. **Cooper Lake III**, 1987
monoprint on rice paper
17 1/2 x 20 7/8

26. **Cooper Lake IV**, 1987
monoprint on rice paper
17 x 21

27. **Leo**, 1987
monoprint on rice paper
17 x 20 5/8

28. **Man Walking in Water**, 1987
monoprint on rice paper
17 x 20 3/4

29. **Man Walking with Orange Leg**, 1987
monoprint on rice paper
21 5/8 x 31

30. **Leaning**, 1987
monoprint on rice paper
17 x 20 7/8

31. **Charles**, 1987
monoprint on rice paper
17 x 20 3/4

Drawings

1. **Swimmer**, 1979
ink on paper
23 1/8 x 35

2. **Woman: Leaning**, 1980
ink and pencil on paper
23 1/8 x 35 1/8

3. **Mayan Head**, 1982
oil on paper
17 1/2 x 14 3/4

4. **Crouching Woman**, 1984
ink on paper
25 3/4 x 37 7/8

5. **Man Standing**, 1985
ink on paper
40 x 26

6. **Man Jumping**, 1985
ink on paper
40 1/8 x 26 1/8

7. **Reclining Woman**, 1985
ink on paper
26 1/8 x 40

8. **Persephone**, 1985
charcoal on paper
35 x 59
Collection of Mr. and Mrs. Ronald W. Moore

9. **Jerusalem**, 1985
ink on paper
25 5/8 x 38

10. **Chimera**, 1986
charcoal and pastel on paper
29 3/4 x 43

11. **Places I Have Been and Memories of Places I Have Never Seen**, 1982-87
mixed media on dry wall tape (scroll)
2 x 243

Shadow Papers

The eight shadow papers in this exhibition were made between 1980 and 1987. They are the following sizes: 12 x 12; 12 x 16 3/4; 12 x 8 3/8; 12 x 17; 12 x 17; 8 1/2 x 10; 12 x 8 1/2; 12 x 10 1/2.

Metal Plates

1. **Tree Fern**, 1983
oil on metal plate
23 7/8 x 26

2. **Poppies**, 1984
oil on metal plate
17 1/2 x 25 1/2

3. **Figures Floating I**, 1985/86
oil on metal plate
47 x 36

4. **Figures Floating II**, 1985/86
oil on metal plate
47 x 36

5. **Landscape with Trees**, 1987
oil on metal plate
20 x 16

Board of Trustees

Lenders to the Exhibition

Mary Frank
Zabriskie Gallery
Mr. Richard Ekstract
The Pennsylvania Academy of the Fine Arts
Everson Museum of Art
Mr. and Mrs. Carter P. Thacher
Leo Treitler
Mr. and Mrs. Ronald W. Moore
Private Collection

Credits

Design: Minelli Design

All page layout and composition executed on the Macintosh Plus computer system

Printing: Davis Press

Photography:
J. Ferrari: pp. 16, 32
Joel Meyerowitz: pp. 7, 70
George Vasquez: pp. 21, 22, 39, 42, 43, 45, 46, 47, 49, 50, 51, 53, 54, 55, 56, 57, 58, 59, 62, 63, 64, 65, 66, 67, 68, 69,
Ralph Gabriner: pp. 1, 13, 17, 19, 26, 29, 31, 33, 34, 35, 36, 37, 38, 41, 44, 48, 52, 60, 61
Sarah Wells: p. 40
Jerry Thompson: pp. 24, 30
Courtesy Zabriskie Gallery: p. 11

This exhibition is accompanied by a videotape produced by Eric Shambroom with technical assistance provided by Video Visuals